HOW TO GET YOUR MESSAGE ACROSS

HOW TO GET YOUR MESSAGE ACROSS

A PRACTICAL GUIDE TO POWER COMMUNICATION

Dr David Lewis

SOUVENIR PRESS

First published 1996 by
Souvenir Press Ltd,
43 Great Russell Street, London WC1B 3PA
and simultaneously in Canada

ISBN 0 285 63348 1 (casebound)
ISBN 0 285 63367 8 (paperback)

Typeset by Rowland Phototypesetting Ltd
Bury St Edmunds, Suffolk
Printed and bound in Great Britain by
Creative Print & Design (Wales), Ebbw Vale

Contents

Acknowledgements

I should like to record my sincere thanks to Cynthia Hemming for her helpful advice and comments about this book in the course of its preparation. My thanks are also due to the following speakers and their companies for permission to quote extracts from their speeches: William A. Andres; Alan Brogan, the Norfolk Southern Corporation; Clive Chajet, Lippincott & Margulies Inc.; W. H. Chrome George, the Aluminum Company of America; John J. McGrath, Argonne National Laboratory; Roger F. Roberts, McDonnell Douglas Corporation; Dr James Todd, American Medical Association; Paul Woollard.

Some of the speech extracts in this book originally appeared in *the Executive Speaker Newsletter*, edited by Robert O. Skovgard. This invaluable resource for speakers can be contacted at PO Box 292437, Dayton, Ohio 45429, USA.

The line drawings are by Richard Armstrong.

While every effort has been made to trace the copyright owners of speeches quoted in this book, should any accidental infringement have occurred the author will be happy to correct such omission in any reprint of the book.

Introduction

Speech is civilisation itself. The word, even the most contra-
dictory word, preserves contact—it is silence which
isolates.

Thomas Mann, *The Magic Mountain*

Great communicators are not born—they are made.

The ability to get your message across, clearly, confidently and persuasively, is a skill which anyone can learn,
practise and perfect.

My purpose in writing this book is to provide you with
a practical guide to the secrets of successful communication. By taking the time and trouble to master the skills
I describe, you will quickly become adept at persuading
others to adopt your ideas, accede to your requests and
accept your point of view.

Even if you are already an experienced communicator
there will still be occasions when you fail to get your
message across as effectively as you hoped. Times when
the words cease to flow and you find yourself incapable
of expressing important ideas as clearly and persuasively

as you want. Moments when you find yourself stumped for the appropriate reply to unexpected objections. Occasions when you fail to persuade listeners to adopt your ideas or agree with your proposals. Times when—and this happens to the very best and most practised of speakers—you find yourself dying on your feet before a critical audience!

All are common traps into which even the best communicators can occasionally fall. Yet even unforeseen hazards can be avoided provided you understand how, when, where and why they are most likely to occur.

If you are currently having difficulty getting your message across, to superiors, colleagues or customers, this book can help transform you into a confident communicator.

The skills you will learn include:

- How to talk fluently and authoritatively—even when there has been little or no time to prepare your comments.
- How to use body language to enhance your spoken words. Did you know, for instance, that there is a simple but powerful piece of body language which virtually *guarantees* that your audience will remember the key part of your message, weeks and months later, without having to take a written note?
- How to prepare messages that will instantly catch and hold the attention of your listeners.
- How to deliver complicated messages either from memory or with a minimum of written notes.
- How to handle media interviews even when dealing with controversial issues.
- How to communicate effectively with audiences from other parts of the world.

A lawyer friend of mine was once asked to defend a surly and recalcitrant prisoner on a charge of drunkenness. After consulting with his client for three hours, he returned to court and apologised that, despite his best endeavours, he was unable to help the court in the matter. 'My client,' he explained, 'may fairly be said to be a man of few words, and so far he has favoured me with only two of them!'

I have met many in business and commerce whose communications skills seemed similarly limited. Sometimes, despite their inarticulacy, they had achieved considerable success in life. More often than not, however, they had failed to achieve their true potential as a result of this inability to get their messages across.

By acquiring the skills and confidence necessary to become an efficient communicator, you can help ensure your career success by making certain you never find yourself lost for words.

CHAPTER 1

Getting Your Message Across

Joy, glory, and magnificence were here for you upon this earth, but you scrabbled along the pavements rattling a few stale words like gravel in your throat, and would have none of them.

Thomas Wolfe, 'Death the Proud Brother'

A TALE OF TWO COMMUNICATORS

Roy and Katherine are computer specialists in their early thirties working for the same software company.

From their résumés it quickly becomes clear that Roy is better qualified. His first class honours degree in mathematics was gained at Oxford while Katherine's second class degree comes from a lower status university. He also has five years' more experience of the commercial world than Katherine, who started her working life as a teacher.

Roy is everybody's idea of a boffin. He is short, bearded

and often scruffily dressed and his eyes shine with intelligence behind thick-rimmed glasses. In the company he has gained the reputation of having an incisive mind and superb analytical skills. He has the knack of getting to the heart of the most complex problems quickly and accurately, coming up with creative solutions to apparently intractable dilemmas.

Although bright and hard working, Katherine is the first to admit she lacks Roy's razor-sharp mind and systems skills. Nor, unlike Roy, could she ever be mistaken for a computer nerd. Tall, elegant and always stylishly dressed, she looks every inch a successful career executive. But those are not the only differences between them.

Although Katherine joined the company three years after Roy, her rise through the management hierarchy has been meteoric. While he seems unlikely to progress much further up the promotional ladder, insiders tip Katherine for the top.

She is already a board-level director frequently called upon to represent her company at major conferences around the world. Whenever they want a spokesperson to talk to press and television, it's invariably Katherine who appears before the microphones and cameras.

Why has this happened?

Quite simply, Katherine is a marvellous communicator. Whatever the situation, no matter how great the pressures or how short the preparation time, she always gets her messages across.

Roy, by contrast, is an utterly ineffective communicator. He stumbles, mumbles and stutters, peppering every sentence with 'ums' and 'ahs'. His voice rarely rises above a barely audible monotone and he has difficulty giving his listeners eye contact. He fidgets, loses track of his ideas and goes into so much unnecessary detail that his key ideas are lost. Even when speaking on a topic of great potential interest to his listeners, Roy manages to bore or baffle them into a state of frustrated indifference.

In the modern business world, being able to communicate clearly, concisely and convincingly has become an increasingly essential calling card for career success.

Even when, like Roy, you possess ample brains, talent, education and experience, an inability to get your messages across is likely to prove a significant barrier to achievement.

COMMUNICATIONS, THE CORPORATE MISSING LINK

Katherines and Roys can be found in virtually all walks of life from the largest corporations and government agencies to the smallest corner stores.

Some people are a joy to talk with: clear, direct and unambiguous in the messages they send to you; thoughtful, reflective and empathic when listening to messages you send to them.

Others, sadly, seem to be followers of Canadian physician Sir William Osler, who advised: 'Look wise, say nothing, and grunt. Speech was given to conceal thought!'

Unfortunately, there are usually many more Roys than Katherines in most organisations. And the problem goes right to the top. Discussing Bill Clinton's communications style, for example, US commentator Tracy Lee Simmons observed that: 'It hardly qualifies as oratory at all. Not only do many of his speeches lack elegance and memorability, they are barely literate.'[1]

In more than thirty years as a professional speaker, broadcaster and trainer, I have met scores of intelligent, highly educated men and women whose communications

1 *National Review*, 6 March, 1995.

styles could fairly be compared to watching paint dry.

The confusions, misunderstandings, mistakes and mis-apprehensions which result from this corporate missing link exact heavy personal and financial penalties on the individuals and organisations concerned.

In a study of 100 companies, The Savage-Lewis Corps of Minneapolis found not only that officials at all levels had difficulty in getting their messages across, but that failures of communication increased with each step down the hierarchy.

At board room level, for example, a senior director talk-ing to another senior director could expect to get 90 per cent of messages across. But when board chairmen talked to their vice-presidents only two-thirds of their communi-cations succeeded. Vice-presidents trying to get their mes-sages across to general managers were successful around half the time (56 per cent). When supervisors talked to workers, however, only one in five messages got through. Reasons for these significant differences in communication success will be described in Chapter Two.

The good news is that it does not have to be like that. As I explained in my introduction, great communicators are not born but made.

You can learn how to get your message across in a way which both informs and persuades your audiences, whether communicating with individual colleagues, small groups, your board of directors or conference audiences.

BOOSTERS AND BARRIERS

When training business people in the art and science of communications, I often hear complaints like: 'I get flus-tered when speaking to a large group' or 'I find it hard to give eye contact while speaking' or 'My voice is not very loud and seems to lack authority.'

Those who express such concerns tend to regard them as weaknesses which, in a sense, they probably often are. Even so, I believe it is unhelpful to regard *any* aspect of the way you get your message across as a problem in and of itself.

In most cases, whether an aspect of your communications style acts as a barrier or a booster depends on a whole host of variables, including the type of message you are trying to get across, the context in which that message is being delivered, the type of audience you are communicating with and your purpose in delivering that communication.

In other words, with the exception of some extremely marked dysfluencies—such as a pronounced stammer—there are no right or wrong ways to get your message across. Let me give you an example of what I mean.

A few years ago I was helping to train salespeople in the pharmaceutical industry. These men and women, who usually have a scientific or medical background, visit doctors in their surgeries to keep them informed of the latest medications.

One of those on my course was an extremely confident and articulate man in his late twenties, whom I will call John. He delivered his sales messages slickly and fluently. In role-playing sessions, where another student would act the part of a stroppy receptionist or hostile medic, he was never disconcerted or lost for words. The other students on the course were both admiring and in awe of him. Without exception, but with varying degrees of success, they all tried to copy John's smooth, self-assured and persuasive communications style.

Nobody wanted to turn herself into John more badly than the youngest student on the course, a diffident and softly spoken former nurse I will call Annie. Her communications style was virtually a mirror image of John's. Where he was confident to the point of brashness, she was shy and quiet. Where he delivered his sales messages fluently and with panache, Annie's pitch was far more hesitant and apologetic. While John's thick skin could deflect the strongest snub and the most discourteous treatment, poor Annie quailed at even the slightest hint of rejection.

Not surprisingly, given their very different temperaments, all Annie's attempts to adopt John's method of getting his message across ended in failure.

After watching these unsuccessful attempts at mimicry over a few workshops, I took Annie aside and suggested she stop trying to become a John clone.

'Be yourself,' I urged. 'Communicate in a way that seems right and comfortable to you.'

'But I'm hopeless when I'm me!' she protested. 'Perhaps I should drop out of the course right now and stop wasting any more of my time or yours. I'll never be able to succeed as a pharmaceutical rep. I'm just not cut out for it.'

I explained that she was being overly defeatist and pessimistic. While there certainly were some barriers to her communications success which needed to be removed, her style also contained plenty of boosters which would greatly assist in getting her message across.

Fortunately Annie allowed herself to be persuaded and completed the course.

Three years later I was a keynote speaker at the company's annual sales conference during which awards were made to their top-performing reps. Top achiever that year, as at the previous conference, was not high flyer John but diffident Annie.

'For the first six months we never thought she would make it,' the sales director told me. 'She didn't seem to be making progress. But the great thing is both the doctors and their receptionists like her quiet and courteous manner. As a result doors open to her more readily than to other, brasher reps. And she builds a warm personal relationship with those who do business with us.'

What Annie had perceived as weaknesses in her communications style were, in fact, strengths given the context in which her messages had to be delivered and the audience (receptionists and doctors) with whom she was talking.

It is essential to regard your own communicating style in the same way. Never automatically consign any aspect of it to the waste can or assume that what appears to be a strength will always help you get your message across.

There can never be a cookbook formula for becoming an effective communicator, because every speaker is different, as are the needs and expectancies of every audience.

Take a slight stutter. This is often regarded as a barrier to successful communication since it slows speech, irritates some listeners and may make it harder for others to understand parts of your message. Yet this same mild dysfluency can help make utterances more memorable and recognisable. Under these circumstances it becomes a booster rather than a barrier to successful communication. It was a slight stammer, for example, which helped make the late Patrick Gordon Campbell a popular UK television personality.

The same can be said for many dialects and accents. In the not so distant past there was a tendency to despise such regional identifiers and insist that the only respectable way to speak English was in the clipped and measured tones of a BBC announcer. Today a wide range of accents and dialects can be heard in broadcasting and among successful professional speakers. Far from detracting from their speech, these variations in tone, sound and inflection are powerful aids to that individual's communications style and success.

Bear in mind, therefore, that there are few hard and fast rules in communicating. All that matters is for your message to be understood clearly, unambiguously and persuasively.

Anything in the way you speak or behave which boosts that process is a plus. Equally, any aspect of your verbal or non-verbal communications style which prevents you getting your message across is a barrier which needs to be dismantled.

Signal and Noise

One way of looking at it is in the engineering sense of 'signal' and 'noise'.

Signal is that part of the transmission which you want your audience to attend to, while 'noise' is any background sound—such as the hissing of static with a weak radio signal—that interferes with comprehension of the message.

Sound engineers concern themselves with the 'signal-to-noise' ratio, and so should you. When this ratio is high your message will get through loud and clear, reducing the risk of misunderstanding and substantially increasing its power to influence and persuade. Where the signal-to-noise ratio is low, however, your audience may be so distracted or confused that your message will fail to get through.

In summary, apart from obvious mistakes, such as an inaudible delivery, incomprehensible diction or inappropriate body language, there are no specifically right or wrong ways to get your message across.

Never be tempted, therefore, to try to copy the style of a speaker you especially admire. What works for him or her will almost certainly not work as well, if at all, for you.

You are a unique individual with your own identity, personality and style as a communicator.

Identify the approach which feels most natural and works best for you, then take time and trouble to develop and perfect this approach.

Not only is this the way to get your message across successfully, it is also the sole means by which you will acquire a personal identity as a communicator.

Identifying Barriers and Boosters

The following questionnaire will help you to identify those aspects of your current communications style which are barriers or boosters, either helping or hindering you in getting your message across.

For the purposes of this assessment I would like you to imagine yourself in each of the situations described and decide which statement best reflects the way you would feel and behave under those circumstances.

Situation 1: Getting Your Message Across to a Large Audience

Imagine you have been asked to make a presentation before a large audience at a major conference. The hall is huge and every seat is taken. From your position on the platform, you look out across a vast expanse of unfamiliar faces, all staring expectantly in your direction. Even if you have never been faced with such a challenge, try to imagine how you would feel in the following situations.

While waiting to be introduced will you be:
a   Slightly apprehensive, but confident of your ability to get your message across effectively;
b   Fairly anxious with a queasy stomach and dry mouth; uncertain that you will be able to communicate your ideas to the large audience;
c   Extremely anxious and confused, with cramped

stomach, sweating palms and trembling hands; certain that you will make a fool of yourself and be utterly humiliated?

Now the moment has arrived. The company chairman has introduced you and, as the audience clap politely, you rise to your feet and start to speak. Will you feel:
a Reasonably relaxed, alert and no more apprehensive about the situation than before you started speaking;
b Far more anxious than a few moments earlier, experiencing surges of panic which make you physically distressed and mentally confused;
c So terrified that you can hardly think what you are saying; certain that everybody in the hall has noticed your nerves; determined to get the terrifying ordeal over as quickly as possible?

While speaking will you be:
a Able to think about what you are saying and reflect on ways you might profitably depart from the prepared text to enliven your delivery and get across your key points more forcefully;
b Obliged to concentrate entirely on the printed text because you feel too anxious about losing your place to depart from the script;
c So anxious and confused you find it hard to read the words clearly and find yourself stumbling and stuttering, frequently losing your place and repeating yourself?

Now the talk is over. As you sit down are you:
a Pleased with the effective manner in which you got your message across;
b Reasonably satisfied but convinced you could have done even better had you been less nervous;

c   Miserable and humiliated by your poor performance
    which meant you failed to get your message across
    successfully?

**Score 1 for each (a), 2 for each (b) and 3 for each (c)
statement ticked.**
Total Score on situation 1 =

Situation 2: Getting Your Message Across to Colleagues

In this situation, imagine you are trying to get your message across to a group of your colleagues. You are having
an informal meeting at which you want to persuade them
to adopt a particular course of action.

As you start speaking are you:
a   Confident you can convince them of the soundness and
    value of your ideas;
b   Hopeful you will be able to persuade them but con-
    cerned at the prospect of handling objections to your
    proposals;
c   Uncertain of winning them around to your point of
    view since experience has shown they seldom adopt
    your ideas?

**When you come to the key points in your proposals do
you:**
a   Present them in such a persuasive manner that the
    others fully appreciate their significance;
b   Do your best to underline the importance of these
    elements in your proposals, but not feel at all certain
    that they fully understand;
c   Make no real attempt to point out their importance
    since they seem to be showing little interest in your
    ideas?

Your colleagues start raising objections. Do you:
a   Listen carefully to the points being made, noting the weaknesses in their objections so as to counter them effectively;
b   Become impatient with what you regard as unreasonable criticisms and refuse to take them seriously;
c   Get thrown off balance by their objections and find it impossible to think up counter-arguments until after the meeting is over?

If those criticisms then increase, will you:
a   Continue countering their objections calmly but firmly;
b   Feel yourself getting so irritated that you bring the meeting to an end before any action has been taken on your ideas;
c   Become so anxious that you concede your proposals are flawed and not worth discussing further?

Score 1 for each (a), 2 for each (b) and 3 for each (c) statement ticked.
Total Score on situation 2 =

Situation 3: Getting Your Message Across to a Superior

You are waiting in the outer office of a superior, or somebody in authority, whose support you must have to carry out your proposals.

In the final moments prior to that meeting do you:
a   Rehearse your arguments and ensure the key elements are firmly fixed in your mind and that you fully understand the supporting evidence;
b   Find it hard to concentrate on your proposals because you feel so concerned about their likely reception;
c   Feel convinced that you will be unable to present your

case sufficiently clearly or convincingly to gain his or her support?

The secretary asks you into the superior's office. While greeting him or her do you:
a Assess your superior's mood and, if necessary, think of a way in which you could modify your arguments to take account of it;
b Observe your superior's mood, feeling thankful if it appears favourable and anxious if it seems hostile;
c Take little or no notice of your superior's mood because you are too busy thinking about what you want to say?

As you present your ideas do you:
a Give your superior eye contact and take notice of his or her body language;
b Have difficulty giving adequate eye contact because doing so increases your anxiety;
c Look anywhere but at your superior because you find it embarrassing to do so?

While summarising the points in favour of your proposals, do you feel:
a You are getting the message across effectively and that you have very likely won his or her support;
b Concerned that you have not presented your case as persuasively as you had hoped;
c It is impossible to tell whether he or she is for or against your proposals?

Reflecting on your meeting afterwards, do you think:
a You put your message across as well as possible and that the case could not have been communicated more clearly;

b   There were one or two weaknesses in the way you got your message across, but your case was generally well argued;

c   It was a waste of time since you had been unable to marshal your arguments effectively or get your message across with sufficient force?

Score 1 for each (a), 2 for each (b) and 3 for each (c) statement ticked.
Total Score on situation 3 =

Situation 4: How You Get Your Message Across

Read all the statements below and, depending on what you said or did the last time you had to deliver an important message, score as follows: seldom or never = 0; occasionally = 1; frequently = 2.

● Mumbled
● Forgot where I was in my presentation
● Gazed at floor or ceiling
● Spoke in a monotone
● Was asked to speak up
● Stumbled over my words
● Fidgeted with a pencil or some other object
● Hesitated and/or used sounds such as 'um' and 'ah'
● Paced the floor
● Sounded unenthusiastic.

Finally total your scores on all four assessments.
Total Score =

What Your Total Score Reveals

Score 50 or more: You have identified several barriers to effective communication. These will have to be removed before you can get your messages across effectively. Once you have mastered the skills described in this book, however, you will find it increasingly easy to communicate in a clear and convincing manner—no matter what situation you find yourself in.

Score 36–49: You are currently encountering some barriers when attempting to get your message across. Work with the techniques I describe to remove these blocks to success while strengthening the positive features of your communications.

Score 21–35: Although you have identified some barriers to successful communication, this score suggests you already have a firm foundation of knowledge and skills on which to build.

Score 20 or less: You clearly have more positive than negative aspects in your communications style and should experience few problems in getting your message across under most circumstances. Use the techniques described in this book to fine tune your already above average level of skills.

Scores on Each Situation

A score of 6 or more on any of the four situations suggests you could be encountering barriers when communicating in a similar situation.

Situation 1 focused on public speaking anxiety which quickly undermines performance.

Situation 2 looked at difficulties which arise when you encounter objections to your proposals.

Situation 3 considered the effects of presenting to individuals of higher status or authority.

Situation 4 explored some of the verbal and non-verbal barriers which arise, partly through anxiety, partly through inexperience and partly from bad habits.

CHAPTER 2

The Magic Bullet of Communications

The unluckiest insolvent in the world is the man whose expenditure of speech is too great for his income of ideas.
Christopher Morley, *Inward Ho*

On 26 June, 1963, John Fitzgerald Kennedy strode out onto a balcony at City Hall, West Berlin. The purpose of President Kennedy's visit was to help boost the morale of the city's beleaguered inhabitants at the height of the Cold War. Before a vast crowd of cheering Germans and the eyes of the world he spoke some of the most famous lines of his political career: 'All free men, wherever they may live, are citizens of Berlin. And therefore, as a free man, I take pride in the words *"Ich bin ein Berliner"*.'

If you watch a newsreel of this historic event, you may notice a momentary start of amazement from the crowd at this stirring proclamation, the briefest of hesitations before they erupted into a frenzy of applause and cheers. Not

21

surprising, really! The President of the United States, one of the most powerful statesmen in the world, had just told his audience that he was a jam doughnut!

What Kennedy meant to say was *'Ich bin Berliner'*. What he actually said, by adding that *'ein'* was something very different.

In this instance it took only a moment for the crowd to understand what he really intended and respond with ecstatic enthusiasm. Other speakers in different circumstances have been less fortunate. All too often the messages they intended to get across proved to be very different from the message their audience heard.

Perhaps something similar has happened to you. You knew what *you* wanted to say. You assumed you had said it. You believed your audience fully understood, only to discover later it had got entirely the wrong idea and responded in a completely different manner from that which you expected.

To understand how things can go wrong we need to look at an apparently straightforward and common-sense theory of how messages are sent and received, one which is sometimes called *The Magic Bullet Theory of Communications*.

In 1948 a man named Harold Laswell defined a communication as 'A process whereby a source transmits a message through some channel to a receiver.'

His idea of the way this process works is illustrated opposite.

First a message is coded in some way. Provided the code can be understood by the intended receiver, its nature is irrelevant. It could just as well be a spoken or written language, Morse code, semaphore, smoke signals or sign language. The code is then transmitted to the receiver along some channel. With the spoken word this comprises changes in air pressure produced by the vocal equipment

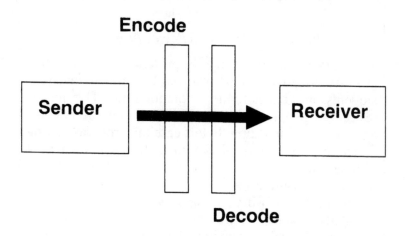

Encode

Sender → **Receiver**

Decode

of the speaker, which stimulate the hearing mechanisms in the ears of the audience.

The receiver decodes the message and understands it clearly and accurately. It's called the Magic Bullet because the information can be thought of as being 'shot' from the brain of one person into the brain, or brains, of others.

Subsequent researchers modified Laswell's definition to include the idea of 'feedback'. That is the verbal or non-verbal response you get from your audience while delivering the message. This clearly will have some influence on how you communicate, not only the content of your message but also the manner in which it is communicated. If you are talking to somebody who seems attentive and interested, you are naturally encouraged to continue. If he or she starts to look bored and begins fidgeting, your inclination may be to stop talking, to shorten your message or to modify it in some way.

Laswell's idea appears so simple, so straightforward and so much in line with how we normally view a communication that even people who have never heard of his Magic

BOX ONE

Feedback: Audience Power in Action

The story is told of an elderly professor of psychology at an American university who was lecturing to first-year students on what is termed 'conditioning'. This means rewarding people, or animals, so that they are encouraged to repeat an action. In this case the Prof was talking about rewarding rats placed in a device known as a Skinner Box, which gives them food pellets in return for their pressing a lever.

The Prof was a dry old stick whose lectures tended to fill the hot lecture theatre with a low, monotonous and sleep-inducing droning. To enliven proceedings, the students decided to see whether they could carry out their own experiment in reinforcement on their lecturer.

He was in the habit of pacing the platform like a caged tiger, striding first to the left and then to the right of the room in a way the students found extremely distracting. He occasionally varied his behaviour by rubbing his left foot against the calf of his right leg.

The students decided to see whether they could 'train' the old chap, without his knowledge, to lecture only from the left side of the platform while standing on one leg. Here's how they set about it.

Each time he moved to the left of the platform he received their full attention; they all looked interested and nodded encouragingly. Every time the poor old professor walked to the right side, however, they averted their gaze, yawned, fidgeted and put on expressions of deep lack of interest.

After a while, so the story goes, the professor—without realising why—could only lecture from the left side of the platform. At that point the students looked inter-

> ested only when he was standing on one leg. In time,
> he always lectured while standing, stork-like, on one
> leg!

Bullet Theory still believe that getting their message across involves this simple process of cause–effect:

Message sent (Cause) --------- Message received (Effect)

'This . . . definition distorts our understanding,' claims Professor Vincent Di Salvo from the University of Nebraska-Lincoln.

> When communication breaks down, some *thing* is
> said to be at fault. Yet communication rarely, if ever,
> lends itself to a single, cause–effect pattern of analy-
> sis . . . it freezes our perspective of communication. It
> assumes that we can lift an instance of communication
> from a given point in time, freeze it, examine it care-
> fully, and thus gain the information we need to under-
> stand the communication process.[1]

In other words, as you may have already discovered to your cost, listeners may fail to fall down when struck by one of your Magic Bullets. Or the gun misfires. Or the bullet turns out to be a blank. Or, despite taking careful aim, you manage to miss your target entirely.

As one corporate speaker remarked wryly after failing to get his message across to the board of directors: 'There's many a slip 'twixt ear and lip!'

'Audiences are obstinate,' agrees Dr R. A. Bauer.

1 Vincent Di Salvo (with Craig Monroe and Benjamin Morse), *Business and Professional Communications*, Charles E. Merrill, Columbus, 1977, pp. 38–9.

They *choose* those with whom they communicate, about what they will communicate, and the meanings that communications come to have for them. If anything, it would appear that the receiver is the active, controlling agent in the communication.[1]

So long as communication is perceived in this appealingly uncomplicated but dangerously misguided way, mistakes are bound to arise. The starting point for getting your message across successfully, therefore, is an understanding of the complex and highly subjective manner in which audiences (whether you are talking to one person or ten thousand) perceive what you are attempting to say.

There are six main barriers which can prevent you from getting your message across effectively.

Barrier 1: Your Message Contains Errors

Even simple mistakes can significantly alter your intended message. A father with a son at private school was sent a letter from the headmaster regretting that due to rising costs, inflation and so on the fees were about to be increased and would, from the next term on, be £5,000 *per anum*. Omitting the 'n' from that Latin phrase certainly changes the meaning of the message!

The father wrote back saying that, if it was all the same to the headmaster, he would sooner continue paying as he had always done: 'through the nose'.

Barrier 2: Your Message Contains Ambiguities

Words often have more than one meaning which can seriously change or distort your intended message. This is exemplified by two famous World War II newspaper head-

1 'The Obstinate Audience: The Influence Process from the Point of View of Social Communication', *American Psychologist*, 19, 1964, pp. 319–28.

lines: 'Monty Flies Back to Front' and 'Americans' Push Bottles Up 5,000 Germans'.

I remember a few years ago a French friend of mine reading a story in the newspaper under the headline 'Mugged English Tourist Critical'. She said this illustrated how remarkably phlegmatic the British were.

'If I had been mugged,' she explained, 'I would not be critical. I would be furious!'

Barrier 3: Key Points of Your Message are Misinterpreted

Unlike readers of a text, your listeners have no chance of turning back a page to re-read anything about which they are unsure.

If something is misinterpreted, the meaning they attached to your message may only come to light when they do or say something inappropriate on the basis of that misinterpretation. Sometimes such a confusion can have catastrophic consequences for those involved.

In 1981, Iqbal Begum was convicted of murdering her husband and sentenced to life imprisonment by a British court. Iqbal spoke no English and her lawyer had relied on translations provided by a Pakistani accountant who acted as interpreter.

At her trial she pleaded guilty, but the judge adjourned the case to make certain she understood the difference between murder, which carries a life sentence, and manslaughter which does not. After confirming through her interpreter that she did understand, Iqbal was sent to prison for life.

Three years later it was revealed that although the accountant was fluent in Gujarati and Hindi, the only language he and Mrs Iqbal had in common was Urdu. The Court of Appeal accepted that, as a native Punjabi speaker,

27

she was not sufficiently proficient in Urdu to understand the difference between murder and manslaughter, despite similarities between the two languages. Her appeal was upheld, the murder conviction quashed and Mrs Iqbal immediately released.[1]

Claire Khatan, a court interpreter for more than twenty years, says that poor interpretation can turn court proceedings from drama to farce: 'Two people are trying to understand each other, but they come from different worlds. They mistakenly think they're communicating, but to anybody who knows both worlds, they're just creating absurdities.'[2]

Sometimes it is not so much the words which lead to the messages being misinterpreted as the context in which they are spoken or written.

Barrier 4: Key Points of Your Message are Misunderstood

Because your listener cannot pause to reflect on a spoken message, it is often helpful to illustrate unfamiliar concepts by means of an anecdote, an analogy or a metaphor (see Chapter Four).

Check your own understanding of somebody else's message using reflective listening (Chapter Three).

Where possible support key verbal messages with written confirmation of the main points.

Your messages may be misunderstood because you incorrectly assume your listener has knowledge of a vital piece of information. Lacking this information, they either cannot understand your instructions or cannot put them into practice (see Box Two).

1 Nuffield Interpreter Project, *Access to Justice*, 1993.
2 *Independent*, 8 May, 1996.

BOX TWO

The Folded Hands Mystery

Here's a conjuring trick which nicely demonstrates how your assumptions about a listener's understanding of your message can lead to misunderstandings.

Explain that you are going to try to teach your listener a simple skill. Say that you will not only explain very carefully what must be done, but also demonstrate it to him or her at the same time to prevent any confusion. You can then add that, despite your best endeavours in getting this message across, around half of those who try to put your instructions into practice are doomed to fail.

Here's what to say and do:

Step 1: Ask the person to stretch his arms out before him. Now tell him to cross his hands over, so the left hand is on the right side of the body and the right hand is on the left (see illustration). Demonstrate this.

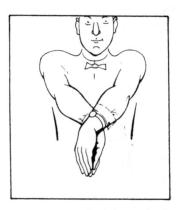

Step 2: Now ask him to interlock the fingers. Demonstrate this.

Step 3: Next he must turn his hands inwards and unlock the first two fingers so they are pointing upward (see illustration). Demonstrate this.

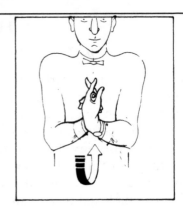

Step 4: Now he is to place one of these fingers on either side of the nostrils (see illustration). Demonstrate this.

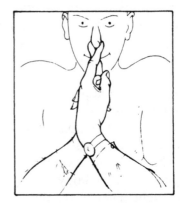

Step 5: The final step is to unlock all the fingers and open up his hands (see illustration). Demonstrate this.

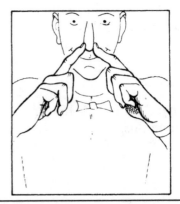

You will find that, no matter how clearly you explain and how carefully you demonstrate these procedures, around 50 per cent of those who attempt to follow your message will get it wrong and be unable to complete step 5.

Why?

Because I failed to make it clear that when the fingers are interlocked in step 2, the *left* thumb must be on top of the right. If the right thumb is on top it is impossible to disentangle your fingers.

Beware of making assumptions and missing out small but vital details when getting your message across.

Barrier 5: Key Points of Your Message are Forgotten

Research suggests that, without written notes and/or visual aids, your audience will remember, after three days, only around 10 per cent of your message. Most likely to be recalled are the things you said first (primacy effect) and the things you said last (recency effect). Unfortunately the key points are often those which come in the middle of a message, the very part where confusion and memory loss are most likely to occur.

In Chapter Twelve I describe a powerful piece of body language you can use when delivering a verbal message to ensure that the 10 per cent your listener recalls includes your key points.

But the best way of enhancing recall is by providing written notes, or, when trying to get your message across to a group, to use slides, overheads, flip charts, or computer-generated graphics, as well as giving hand-outs to those present.

Barrier 6: Your Messages are Interpreted Subjectively

Perhaps because this barrier is the most subtle, it is also the one most frequently overlooked by people trying to get their messages across.

Even though they have managed to avoid the other five, they fail to communicate in the way they expected because their listener(s) heard not *what* was said but what they *thought* was said.

This barrier arises because every message we receive is filtered through a prism made up of the sum total of our experiences, background, education, knowledge, biases, prejudices, hopes, fears, dreams, dreads, loves, loathings, likes, dislikes, wishes, superstitions, expectations and emotional states at the moment the information is delivered.

When Harry Cale[1] moved from another company to take

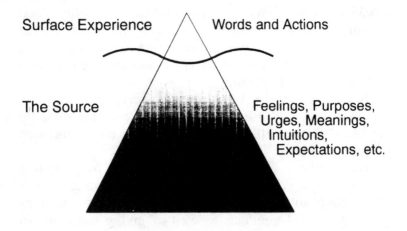

Surface Experience   Words and Actions

The Source   Feelings, Purposes, Urges, Meanings, Intuitions, Expectations, etc.

1 Names have been changed.

up his appointment as vice-president in charge of personnel at Grotto Inc., he was determined to be looked on as a friend, somebody the workforce could turn to in times of trouble. To get this message across he sent around a 'My door is always open' memo inviting them to meet him at any time.

Many of the employees, who had expected the existing personnel manager to be promoted to the vacancy, felt uncertain and somewhat threatened by Cale's surprise appointment. They interpreted this memo as a strategy to gain leverage over them.

However, one supervisor, a charge-hand we will call Bob Smith, decided to take up Cale's offer and was given an 11 o'clock appointment. Arriving on time, he was irritated to be kept waiting until 11.25 without explanation or apology.

When finally ushered into Cale's office, Bob saw a large and imposing mahogany desk, a plush carpet, panoramic windows high above the street, oil paintings on the wall and the V-P's expensively tailored suit. In his factory-floor overalls, Smith, not surprisingly, felt uncomfortable and intimidated.

Cale was signing letters when his visitor was shown in and continued doing so without looking up. As a result Bob had to stand for several minutes before being invited to sit down.

While they chatted, the new V-P's tone and manner were pleasant enough, but their conversation was constantly interrupted as he took telephone calls and gave instructions to his secretary.

After fifteen minutes of irrelevant small talk, Bob Smith left the vice-president's office feeling patronised and humiliated by the encounter, an experience he vowed never to repeat.

Cale, by contrast, felt confident he had got his message

of openness through to the employee and forged useful links to the shop floor.

Getting your message across is never simply a matter of creating a 'shopping list' of needs and expectations. Just as important is where, when, how and with whom that message is communicated.

THE PYRAMID OF PERCEPTION

Two types of information are involved in our perception of the world.

The first, which has been termed Information 1, consists of all the information reaching our brain at any given moment; in other words everything to which our senses have access.

Information 1 does not impose any objective reality on us, but is 'made sense of' only in terms of Information 2. This comprises everything which makes each of us a unique human being, our experiences, expectations, hopes, dreams, ambitions, desires, fears, likings, loathings, prejudices, presumptions, storehouse of knowledge and prior learning experiences.

It also includes our state of mind (alert/fatigued, angry/calm, anxious/relaxed, drunk/sober, depressed/happy, worried/at ease, etc.) at the time the message is delivered.

Our emotions are especially important since all incoming messages are first processed by that part of the brain responsible for feelings before being passed on to higher regions for more objective analysis.

As a result, only a fraction of the total content of a message, comprising not only the words themselves but everything present in both our external and internal environments (i.e. body language, our surroundings, our mental states, etc.), reaches the regions of conscious attention. Other information affects us, often powerfully, below the level of awareness while still further information is simply ignored. Called the 'bow tie' of communications, this is illustrated below.

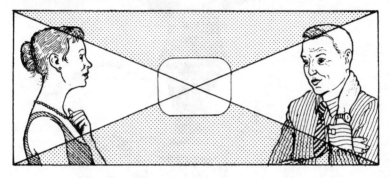

Three elements exert the greatest influence over a listener's subjective assessment of your message:

1 Personal Relevance
2 Selective Attention
3 Selective Perception.

Personal Relevance

For most of us, most of the time, the most important person in our lives is—US!

As a result, we naturally pay greatest attention to messages which appear to have the most personal relevance.

In one study of astrology, for instance, some subjects were given general descriptions of their personalities based on star signs. Others received descriptions the researchers claimed were based on the exact hour, day, month and year of each individual's birth. Those who thought the profile referred uniquely to them were far more likely to believe it than those told it applied to everybody born under their star sign.

35

Imagine you are about to fly off on holiday. As the aircraft taxis down the runway in preparation for take-off the cabin crew go through the safety precautions. They point out the exits, indicate where the emergency lighting strips are along the cabin floor, explain where oxygen masks will appear in case of depressurisation and demonstrate how to use the life-jackets.

Does anybody ever really look or listen while this is going on?

In my experience, and that of most of the flight attendants I have talked to, hardly anyone bothers.

Psychologically there are three good reasons for this.

The first is anxiety. The last thing people want to think about when taking off is the prospect of not coming safely back to earth again. So passengers bury their heads in books and magazines or carry on chattering to their neighbours as the messages are delivered.

Second, people dislike other passengers seeing them as first-time flyers. Frequent travellers demonstrate their familiarity with the safety instructions by ignoring them. Inexperienced passengers, wishing to seem knowledgeable, do the same.

But the third reason is, perhaps, the most important of them all. Passengers see no personal relevance in the ritual. The message fails to get across because it fails to take account of the WIIFM factor.

WIIFM stands for What's In It For Me? It has been described as the world's most popular radio station since we are all tuned into it at every waking moment of our lives.

To see how WIIFM works in practice, consider our blasé airline passengers at 37,000 feet above the Atlantic. The captain suddenly announces that, due to a sudden failure of the hydraulic systems, he must attempt a crash landing in the ocean. Faced with this emergency, those aboard will suddenly become very interested in knowing where the exits are and how to use their life-jackets.

Communications which take an audience's WIIFM factor into account stand a far stronger chance of getting through than those which are seen as having little or no personal relevance.

Which of the following messages about crime, for example, would you be more likely to take notice of?

Version 1: Crime statistics just released show domestic burglary is soaring. It is fast becoming the most common of all crimes, with one householder in four being at risk of having their homes broken into during the next six months. For those living in inner-city areas, the chances of becoming a robbery victim rise to one in two. Yet conviction rates remain low, with less than one robbery in a hundred ending in a conviction.

Not only are items which are often of only sentimental value stolen, but the new breed of burglars often wilfully vandalises property, smashing ornaments, defacing walls and soiling carpets.

Version 2: Crime statistics just released show domestic burglary to be soaring. It is fast becoming the most common of all crimes, with *your* chances of being robbed over the next six months being one in four.

If *you* live in an inner-city area, *your* chances of being a robbery victim rise to one in two.

Yet the chances that the person who broke into *your* house will be convicted are less than one in a hundred. Not only will *you* lose items of sentimental value but the new breed of burglar will often wilfully vandalise *your* property, smashing *your* ornaments, defacing *your* walls and soiling *your* carpets.

Communication can be described as *an effort after meaning*. The significance of any message lies as much in what the individual brings to the situation as to the message itself.

Take the case of managers seeking to get an important message across to their workforce. They spend a lot of time debating the best method of communicating their views.

Should a conference be called, or a video produced?

Would it be sufficient to publish the new policy in the company newsletter or convey it via e-mail?

The truth is it does not usually matter which medium is used. All can be equally effective when the workforce is highly motivated to receive that message and equally ineffective if they are antagonistic towards it.

In summary, the more personally relevant you can make any message the stronger its chances of being listened to carefully and acted upon promptly.

DROWNING IN A SEA OF INFORMATION

When the nineteenth-century psychologist William James described the world as a 'booming, buzzing, confusion' he wasn't far wrong.

We are swimming in an ocean of information. And if it sometimes feels as if we are drowning rather than swimming this is hardly surprising.

Some 10,000 potential sensory impressions *per second*, or 288 million impressions in the average working day[1] are available to us. Unfortunately our brain is capable of attending to no more than 500 bits of information per second.[2]

By attending, I mean the process by which we bring specific items of information into sharp and vivid focus, while allowing other items to recede and grow fuzzy until they fall below the level of conscious awareness.

To cope with the drastic imbalance between potentially

1 R. Watzlawick, J. H. Beavin and D. D. Jackson, *The Pragmatics of Human Communication*, New York, W. W. Norton, 1967.
2 W. V. Haney, *Communication and Organisational Behavior*, 3rd edition, Homewood, Illinois, Irwin, 1973.

available information and the brain's processing capacity we are obliged to be highly selective about what we notice and what we choose to ignore. All incoming information must compete for attention, rather like children in a huge family who constantly clamour and yell to catch their parents' eye. The two processes by which this is achieved are selective attention and selective perception.

Selective Attention

To survive in the world we must first make sense of it. To make sense of it we must have information, which is provided via our senses. To understand what we are seeing, hearing, smelling, tasting or touching we select useful cues from the information available and organise it into meaningful patterns. This process is illustrated below.

To make sense of this image you must first discriminate among the collection of apparently random blots and splotches before organising that information into a meaningful form. Once you have done this a picture will spring off the page at you, and what previously looked like a meaningless array of marks will be transformed into a clear image, which, ever after, will immediately appear each time you look at the illustration.[1]

The drawing below illustrates selective attention in action.

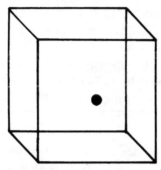

This is called a Necker Cube, after the nineteenth-century geologist who first recognised the phenomenon while studying line drawings of crystals in a text book. Look steadily at the dot and the cube will abruptly change shape (if this doesn't seem to be working for you, try blinking). Continue staring and it will alter its shape once again. After the first few changes you will find the switching occurs with increasing frequency.

The change is what mathematicians call *discontinuous*, since there is no intermediate stage between one shape and the next—it just flips straight over.

This happens because the image is ambiguous. The

1 Still having trouble making sense of the picture? Try looking for a Dalmatian.

BOX THREE

The Cocktail Party Phenomenon

Chatting to somebody at a cocktail party provides an excellent practical example of selective attention in action. Without much difficulty you are able to close your ears to all the other simultaneous conversations and focus all your attention on that one person.

At some level, however, it appears you are still aware of what else is being said, since if anyone speaks your name, you will almost always hear it and switch your attention to him or her.

The same thing happens if an obscenity is spoken, only this time everybody is likely to hear it, stop talking and stare at the person concerned!

---

information it provides can be interpreted in a number of equally correct ways. It is as if your visual centres 'say' to the higher regions of thought: 'One way of looking at this object is this ... another way is that. You make up your mind which is correct!'

When confronted by a message which may be interpreted in a number of ways, the same situation is likely to occur and can act as a barrier to effective communication. You believe you said one thing; your audience believes you said something completely different, and acts accordingly.

Selective attention occurs at fairly low levels in the brain, where decisions are made as to which of the incoming messages will be allowed to pass into the higher regions of thought for consideration and which will be censored out from awareness. This does not mean, of course, that they will not be perceived and acted upon at a subconscious level. Indeed, many of the judgements we make and actions we take are determined by feeling based on information forever banished to the subconscious realms of the mind.

Five types of message are most likely to get past this censor and be selected for conscious consideration.

1   Messages which, for any reason, stand out from the masses of information surrounding us. This effect is illustrated below:

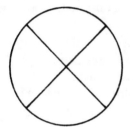

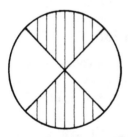

Because the first figure lacks any single, discernible pattern, the eye wanders over it haphazardly. Blink and the chances are your perspective will change.

The second figure immediately draws your attention to the vertical lines within the circle since they stand out clearly from the background.

A company which circulates hundreds of memos to its executives may fail to communicate important messages if they look no different from trivial, unessential, routine memos.

2   Messages especially relevant to our current needs. When we feel hungry, for instance, far more importance is attached to, and more notice taken of, messages relating to food. Moral: never go shopping for food on an empty stomach or you will probably end up buying more than you need and much that you don't need!

3   Messages consistent with our beliefs, values and attitudes.

4   Messages which include novel or unexpected information. This has long been exploited by tabloid headline writers. Few, I suspect, could resist reading a story headlined 'Freddie Starr Ate My Hamster' (the *Sun*) or 'London Bus Found on Moon' (*Sunday Sport*).

Selective attention means that: 'When we attach meaning to a situation, we abstract a portion of the Information 1 available to us in terms of the unique blend of Information 2 that we bring to bear on it.'[1]

Selective Perception

Just as we see what we expect to see, so too do we perceive what we expect to perceive. As we learn about something (an individual, group, social class, object, etc.), we build expectations about it.

Such expectations, which are frequently associated with beliefs, stereotypes, attitudes, emotions and feelings, 'prepare us to respond to an object of our perception in a particular way. As our expectations become stronger, alternative responses become less and less likely.'[2]

1 Vincent Di Salvo, *op. cit.*, p. 44.
2 Vincent Di Salvo, *op. cit.*, p. 47.

In one early experiment in the United States,[1] subjects were given three different messages about the bussing issue. At that time bussing was a highly controversial measure which involved transporting children by bus to specified schools in order to achieve a racial balance.

One of these messages was strongly in favour of the practice, the second strongly opposed, while the third offered balanced arguments for both sides. These messages were attributed either to Martin Luther King, Jr, or to Governor George Wallace, a racist and notorious segregationist.

When the pro-bussing message was attributed to Martin Luther King it was seen as significantly more favourable than when attributed to Wallace.

Similarly the anti-bussing message was seen as being more unfavourable to bussing when attributed to Wallace than to King. But the most interesting findings centred on the evenly balanced third message.

When attributed to Martin Luther King this was perceived as being very strongly pro-bussing; when attributed to Wallace as being violently anti-bussing.

Remember the messages did not change, only the receivers' perceptions of those messages.

To test the effect of expectation on perception for yourself, try this exercise.

Cover the numbers overleaf with a sheet of paper. Move the paper downward to reveal them one at a time and count the numbers aloud as you do so, i.e. 'One thousand, two thousand, two thousand and twenty, three thousand and twenty', etc.

1 J. W. Koehler, J. C. McCroskey and W. E. Arnold, *The Effects of Receiver's Constancy Expectation in Communication*, Research Monograph, Department of Speech, Pennsylvania State University, 1966.

1000
1000
20
1000
40
1000
30
1000
10

Was your final total 6000? If so you have responded in the way the majority does when asked to perform this calculation.

The right answer is 5100.

So why do so many people get it wrong? Because in the few seconds it took to do the addition, your mind had been locked into a mind set which geared you to think in thousands. It is hardly surprising therefore that expectations set up over a lifetime's experiences should exert an even more powerful effect on our perceptions.

Summary

Although it appears no more than simple common sense, the Magic Bullet Theory acts as a barrier to getting a message across.

It leads us to believe that, provided we understand what we want to say, and then say it, others will interpret our communication in exactly the same way.

It also means that if a message fails to get through we may look for some simple cause–effect explanation. However, the situation is too complex for such an analysis to produce any useful answers.

Bear in mind that attention and perception are highly selective and subjective.

To persuade or inform, ensure that your message contains a strong WIIFM factor and is presented in a way which enables your audience to pick up on the factor quickly and easily.

The earlier on in your message you explain exactly how and why it is important to your listeners, the more likely they are to pay attention to the whole communication.

CHAPTER 3

The Winning Power of Words

Haven't you learned yet that I put something more than
whisky into my speeches?
              Winston Churchill to his son Randolph

One fine May morning a few years back, a friend of mine
named Andy Gibbens was crossing New York's Central
Park on his way to a job interview in Madison Avenue.
In spite of the fine day and the beauty of his surroundings,
Andy's mood was grim and his mind preoccupied with
worries as he hurried towards his appointment. Around
him trees and flowers were blooming and sunlight glim-
mered on the waters of the lake, but Andy saw nothing of
this. All his thoughts were on the interview ahead. Six
months earlier Andy, a gifted and experienced creative in
his late twenties, had been made redundant from his job
with a top advertising agency.

At first he hadn't worried too much about mounting
bills and declining savings. Hard working and talented,

Andy felt confident of quickly finding another job. But the recession had bitten deep into the advertising heartland and, despite a score of interviews and hundreds of phone calls, half a year later he remained unemployed. Andy was deeply in debt and knew that unless he was successful at this interview he would be in serious financial trouble.

As he climbed the steps out of Central Park, my friend's attention was caught by a sight which put his own problems into perspective. A man of about his own age sat begging on the park wall. Propped up beside him was a notice, handwritten on a scrap of board, which read 'I AM BLIND!' This plea was clearly failing to move the hearts of New Yorkers and tourists bustling past. Apart from a scattering of nickels and dimes the begging bowl was empty.

Moved by this sad spectacle, and reflecting on how much the unfortunate young man was missing on such a beautiful day, my friend went over to him.

'I can't afford to give you any cash,' he explained apologetically. 'I've been out of work myself for months. But, if you agree, I can help you in a different way. I'd like to make a few changes to your notice.'

Surprised, the beggar hesitated for a moment before shrugging. 'Sure, do what you like. But I'm telling you it will take a hell of a message to make the folk in this city take pity on another beggar.'

Andy took a marker pen from his pocket, added three words to the notice and went on his way.

Three hours later he was returning home via Central Park. This time his step was light and his footsteps brisk. The interview had been successful, the job was his and very soon his financial worries would be over.

Passing the beggar he was delighted to see his new message had proved effective at opening the hearts and wallets of passers-by. The bowl was overflowing with gifts, not just nickels and dimes but five and ten dollar bills.

49

'You're doing a whole lot better,' he told the man.

'I sure am,' the beggar replied. Then, recognising Andy's voice, he asked in bewilderment, 'How did you change my message to make so much difference to my fortunes?'

Andy replied, 'I just added three words. Now it reads: "I AM BLIND—AND IT'S SPRING".'

I often recount that story at workshops on communications because it illustrates not just the tremendous power of words to move and motivate us, but also the crucial importance of creating messages which persuade as well as inform, which appeal to the emotional first brain as well as the logical, analytical regions of thought.

When preparing any type of important message always begin by asking yourself the following three questions:

1   What is my purpose in communicating this message; what do I want it to accomplish?
2   What do my listeners need to know for that purpose to be accomplished?
3   How much time shall I have to get my message across to them?

Relating back to the blind man's slogan, we can see how the second version succeeded where the first, informative message failed.

1   What is the purpose of my sending this message; what do I want it to accomplish?

Clearly the purpose was to arouse sympathy for the blind man's plight in order to *persuade* busy, preoccupied and probably cynical passers-by to open their hearts and their wallets to him.

2   What do my listeners need to know for that purpose to be accomplished?

Just being made aware of the beggar's disability was

clearly not enough. The coldly clinical statement 'I AM BLIND' does nothing to get across the message of what it is *like* to be blind, how it feels to miss out on sights which others take for granted.

The message had to be changed if it was to gain first the attention of passers-by and then their sympathy. The most effective form of words could be reached only when the third question had been answered . . .

3 How much time shall I have to get my message across to them?

In this case the answer was clearly only a few seconds, the time it would take New York pedestrians—among the fastest movers in the world—to hurry by.

No time, therefore, to write at length on how it feels to inhabit a world of utter darkness, as the seventeenth-century poet John Milton did about his blindness:

> When I consider how my light is spent,
> E're half my days, in this dark world and wide,
> And that one Talent which is death to hide,
> Lodg'd with me useless . . .

Despite its beauty and eloquence, this message would have stood little chance of being read at all, let alone persuading distracted and uninterested strangers to lend a helping hand.

Andy's additional comment could scarcely have been shorter or more to the point. Yet those few words 'AND IT'S SPRING' were all it took to change information which registered only with the brain to a phrase which touched the heart. In terms of getting the blind man's plight across it proved a perfect message.

It also illustrates the three components every effective

communicator must take into account when deciding how to get his or her messages across.

THE THREE A'S OF EFFECTIVE COMMUNICATIONS

To communicate effectively you have to possess:

- Awareness—of your audience's needs
- Attention—to the structure of your message
- Anxiety management—skills which enable you to remain calm and in control even when trying to get across controversial messages in the face of reluctant or hostile audiences.

Without consideration of these factors your message has a far higher risk of failing either to get through at all or, having got through, to produce the desired effect on your listener(s).

In this chapter we shall be exploring the first of these components.

AWARENESS OF YOUR AUDIENCE'S NEEDS

How do you know what type of message will have the greatest effect on those with whom you communicate?

In most cases the simple answer is to listen and look. Preferably you should listen and look *before* structuring your message in order to ensure it stimulates their WIIFM factor. Certainly you must listen and look while delivering the message in order to receive feedback that lets you know whether or not the message is getting across. And you should continue listening and looking during any follow-ups, such as a question and answer session, to your message.

Later in this chapter I will be describing some of the

non-verbal signs which can reveal a great deal about how an individual likes to be talked to. In Chapter Twelve I will describe some of the subtle body-language signals which allow you to detect interest or inattention. But we'll start by considering what many regard as a lost art in our high-pressure, fast-paced society—the art of listening.

How to Become a Professional Listener

A wise person once said we have two ears and one mouth and should always use them in that ratio, listening twice as much as speaking. As the nineteenth-century historian Thomas Carlyle put it: 'Under all speech that is good for anything there lies a silence that is better.'

Hearing and listening are not one and the same. All those fortunate enough to possess healthy, well-functioning auditory mechanisms can hear, but it takes practice to learn how to listen.

One problem is that our brain is able to process speech far more rapidly than people usually talk. During normal conversation we often speak at a rate of fewer than 100 words per minute, and a racing commentator flat out seldom exceeds 200 words per minute. Yet our brain is capable of making sense of words spoken more than twice as fast.

Adding to the risk of our becoming distracted, conversations are usually riddled with repetitions, the same idea being stated and restated many times, often with only slight variations. The conversational mix also includes meaningless or redundant sounds and phrases such as 'umm . . . er . . . mmmm' and 'you know', 'you see', 'like' and 'I mean'.

The next time you listen to a radio or television interview, notice how often an interviewee starts his answer with 'Well', frequently followed by a pause. The word and the silence provide an extra second or so of thinking time in which the speaker can formulate an answer. Incidentally the use of these sounds and phrases illustrates another crucial point about the usefulness of silence when getting your message across. Being able to stay quiet for a few moments instead of rushing to fill the silence with sound—any old sound—is a key communicating skill and one which I discuss further in Chapter Seven.

Slow speech, repetition, redundancy and meaningless sounds cause all but the most practised listeners to switch their attention away from what is being said onto some more interesting thought. Yet if you allow your attention to wander you run the risk of false assumptions and significant misunderstanding.

Avoid this trap by active listening. While continuing to pay close attention to what is being said, silently ask yourself questions: 'How do those comments affect the way I should structure my message?' 'In what ways could that opinion influence the way I get my message across?' 'Who else in my audience might hold the same views?'

These unspoken questions enable you to check your understanding of what's said in addition to making key points easier to remember. Listen for hesitations, pauses, silences and changes in the emphasis or speed of delivery, since these may reveal strong emotions beneath the seemingly calm surface of a person's conversation, emotions which may betray far more about that individual's feelings on the subject than the words he or she speaks.

Careful, attentive listening is vital if you are to understand what motivates and drives your listeners and, consequently, the type of messages to which they will prove most and least receptive. It will also often provide you with clues to how best to get your message across by identifying the type of communication with which they feel most comfortable. This is an important benefit of active listening and one which I shall deal with in detail below.

Barriers to Active Listening

The first barrier is the mistaken belief that you can do two things at once.

You are working on an important project, for example, when a colleague comes over to discuss a different topic. Instead of stopping what you are doing and giving her your full attention, you listen with half an ear while attempting to carry on your original task. Now and then you may nod, give brief eye contact or mutter noises of agreement simply to appear polite. But your focus remains on your project and you only have a vague idea of what she is saying.

Such distracted listening happens most frequently when we are being introduced to somebody for the first time. Instead of paying attention to his name and other personal details, we are distracted by wondering what sort of a person he is; whether we find him physically attractive or unappealing; whether he can help further our careers; whether he is bright or unintelligent, interesting or dull, fun or dreary; whether or not he likes us, is interested in us or attracted to us and so on.

This is the main reason why so many people have so much difficulty remembering the name of someone to whom they were introduced only moments before.

They can't recall that information because they never really listened, only vaguely heard what was said.

President Franklin D. Roosevelt believed people never really listened to what he said to them and only heaped praise on his comments from politeness. To test this theory he sometimes greeted his guests: 'So good to see you. I murdered my grandmother this morning!'

On most occasions the other person replied politely and approvingly. He was only caught out once when a woman to whom he had addressed this confession nodded sym-

---

BOX FOUR

What's in a Name?

A public relations executive was given the task of 'rescuing' a client company from the bad publicity being created by a journalist with a vendetta against it. To set the record straight the client offered the journalist an 'exclusive' interview with the company's managing director.

When the journalist arrived, the PR executive was struck by how rodent-like his features seemed. Unfortunately this thought slipped out and he introduced him to his client as Mr Weasel. The indignant journalist later took his revenge by writing a scathing article. Soon after, the PR company lost the account.

---

pathetically and responded: 'Mr President, I'm sure she had it coming to her!'

Avoid falling into the trap of distracted listening by deciding your priorities. If your current task takes precedence, explain politely but firmly you do not have time to listen at that moment, and arrange an appointment when you will be able to give the speaker your undivided attention. Far from being upset he'll feel flattered that you take him seriously.

When he obviously has something crucially important to say, stop what you are doing, set the work aside and listen carefully.

Red Buttons and Green Flags

Never attempt to listen actively when you are feeling angry, anxious, upset or in any other state of high emotional arousal.

Strong emotions can be as much a barrier to listening

as being distracted by an attempt to do two things at once. This is often an important reason for misunderstandings and mistakes in messages between people of different status. Apprehension about communicating with somebody viewed as considerably more powerful and important than yourself tends to tie your tongue and block up your ears.

We also all have what I call our little red buttons. These are the opinions or attitudes of others which trigger an emotional reaction within you, a reaction which can sometimes be so powerful it overwhelms you.

Manipulative people sometimes deliberately try to press one of your red buttons in order to gain a psychological advantage. Whenever you feel your emotions taking command, inhale deeply and slowly count up to five while breathing out. As you do so, say firmly but silently, '*Stop!*'

Since it is impossible to hold in mind more than one thought at a time, your emotional reaction will, at least for a moment, be brought under control. This technique can also be used during diagnostic listening (see below)

If you still feel too upset to listen objectively, take a break from the conversation. Even a short pause can make all the difference to the attention you can bring to that exchange.

What I term green flags, which consist of praise and compliments, are another emotional trap. While far more agreeable than red buttons, they can be no less disruptive. Flattery tunes in the WIIFM factor and tunes out other, perhaps more significant and less palatable, aspects of the message.

Safeguard yourself against the green flag trap by first acknowledging the complimentary remarks and then tactfully moving the conversation to a neutral topic until you have regained your composure.

Postpone listening to emotionally charged messages until you have calmed down and can assess the situation

---

BOX FIVE

We Hear What We Want to Hear

A businessman and a naturalist were strolling down a busy city street. The naturalist paused by an overgrown building site. 'Listen,' he said delightedly. 'Do you hear that cricket?'

The businessman shook his head, then, glancing towards the hurrying crowd, added, 'And neither does anyone else!'

Taking a coin from his pocket, the naturalist let it drop to the pavement. At the faint clink of metal on stone a dozen heads immediately turned. 'What you hear,' he explained quietly, 'depends on what you want to hear.'

---

objectively before attempting to listen. Even a short break can make a big difference to the care and attention you can bring to what is said.

Another common trap is to listen dismissively because you've already decided that the person has nothing worthwhile to say.

Dismissive Listening

This occurs whenever you've made up your mind about what another person is trying to say. As a result you pay attention only to information which confirms your first impression and dismiss everything else as irrelevant or unimportant. Either way you will almost certainly fail to identify and satisfy the other's WIIFM factor.

Avoid falling into the trap of dismissive listening by approaching every verbal communication with an open mind and not making assumptions or prejudgements.

Use diagnostic and reflective listening (see below) to

establish exactly what message the other person is seeking to get across.

Judgemental Listening

This happens whenever you pass judgement on somebody's message before anything much has been said. The risk of judgemental listening increases whenever we try to fit people into convenient pigeonholes.

For example, assumptions that all tall people are assertive, all stocky individuals are unambitious, redheads possess hot tempers and people who wear glasses have above average intelligence can have a powerful influence over how we judge their communications.

When speaking to a person pigeonholed as having a very high IQ we will afford even the most trivial remark a degree of respect denied to those whose IQ we assume to be meagre.

You can avoid this listening trap by means of the empathic listening technique described below.

Although I have described these forms of listening separately, they are seldom so easy to separate in everyday life. Distracted listening may lead you to make judgements about another person which result in your listening to them dismissively. Equally, forming a negative judgement about the significance of what you are told quickly produces distracted listening.

The Power of Positive Listening

There are three forms of positive, active listening.

Diagnostic Listening

Remain non-judgemental. Any comments, especially critical ones, increase people's reluctance to talk about deeper concerns. This makes it far harder for you to identify their true feelings, motives or needs.

Pay attention to voice tone. Any conflict between what and how words are spoken can reveal powerful emotions below the surface.

Be on the alert for self-deprecating jokes. People often use humour to protect themselves against rejection or embarrassment.

Study expression, gestures and posture. Bodily tension, especially when combined with fidgets, indicates stress.

Notice lengthy pauses, hesitations or repetitions which may also betray anxiety. Pay attention to *parapraxes*, Freud's term for slips of the tongue. These may reveal subconscious feelings about somebody or something.

Use what is called the PIN approach for extracting further information, ideas or comments. This means starting by focusing on anything Positive in their proposals. Next consider Interesting aspects and only then turn to Negative aspects of their proposals.

Reflective Listening

On occasions you will find it helpful to paraphrase and repeat back what you have just been told. It confirms whether or not you have fully understood the message, so preventing mistakes and misapprehensions. Where any misunderstanding has occurred, reflective listening catches it before any harm is done.

It also helps identify errors in the message itself. Until he has his ideas repeated back, the speaker may be unaware of their implications.

Reflective listening also reduces the emotional attachment a speaker has to his or her particular ideas. By placing them in the 'public arena' you make it easier for the speaker to put the proposals into perspective.

While not every utterance should be reflected back, try to do this with key concepts and complex ideas.

Empathic Listening

Try to put yourself in the other person's position, seeing the situation through her eyes and hearing it through her ears.

Empathic listening enables you to identify an individual's favoured style of communication, based on her use of language and eye movements, as I describe below:

When listening keep six basic rules in mind:

1 Before embarking on any form of communication, have a clear idea of what you hope, or expect, to achieve.
2 Gain a psychological advantage by initiating conversations. Whoever starts the communication is better able to direct it along the lines they wish.
3 Smooth the way for people who are reticent, shy or rather inarticulate, by interjecting encouraging comments such as 'I see' or 'I understand'. At the same time smile, nod, give adequate, but not overpowering eye contact and look interested.
4 Check your understanding of their message by asking, Who? What? When? Where? Why? How?
5 Listen for pauses, hesitations or repetitions, all of which can reveal anxiety.
6 Talk less than you listen and you'll find it far easier

61

to get your own message across when your turn comes to speak.

Summary

- Listening and hearing are different abilities. Positive listening must be learned and practised.
- Avoid listening in a distracted, dismissive or judgemental manner. Keep an open mind.
- Be aware of red buttons—words said which trigger powerful emotions. And beware green flags since praise sometimes deafens you to criticisms.
- Positive listening can be diagnostic, reflective or empathic.
- Listen below the surface of words. Crucial parts of the message are often communicated in pauses, emphases and hesitations.

How Words Betray Motives

You can learn a great deal by listening to the way other people strive to communicate. Since you are more likely to trigger somebody's WIIFM factor if you use the sort of words, phrases and sentences they feel most comfortable using, such insights could mean the difference between being listened to and failing to get your message across.

There are four main types of communicator: Masterminds, Mothers, Mechanics and Motivators.

Masterminds

'My plan for the company is straightforward,' CEO Chris Driver tells fellow directors at their annual general meeting. 'Our goals are in sight, our objectives clearly stated, the way ahead is plain . . .'

This is the language of a Mastermind, who can, of

course, be of either sex. Such people tend to be ambitious high-achievers who set firm goals in life and work single-mindedly towards their accomplishment.

They tend to see themselves as natural leaders to whom others will turn for direction and guidance. Masterminds are often workaholics, prepared to sacrifice family and social relationships to reach the top. They are typically the first to arrive and the last to leave the office. They are always on the go and impatient to get on with their lives.

To get your message across to a Mastermind, use the language of accomplishment and ambition. Include phrases such as: 'The purpose of this project . . .', 'see how these ideas will open up new frontiers', 'achieving these targets will ensure that . . .'

Mothers

Again this is intended to describe either gender. Mothers use the language of feelings and intuitions: 'My gut reaction to this scheme,' explains teacher Vivian Love to colleagues, 'is that it will hurt the very people it is intended to help. I feel very strongly that we risk emotionally harming those least able to defend themselves. Intuitively one senses the pain this will cause, even before the plans have been implemented.'

Phrases and words like this are mostly chosen by 'people people' who get on best and are happiest when dealing with other human beings rather than working with things.

Warm, empathic and intuitive, they have a sympathetic understanding of others which makes them skilled negotiators and mediators.

To get your message across to them, use the language of mediation and compromise. Do not be afraid to talk about your hunches and intuitions. Do not be afraid to allow your emotions to show through when discussing issues about which you have strong feelings. While such an approach would be anathema to the goal-directed Mastermind, it will strike a resonant chord with Mothers.

Mechanics

As before they can be of either sex. Sam Practical is discussing plans for a community project to build a children's playground in their neighbourhood: 'It will take six weeks to complete, and require around two tons of bricks, a ton of sand and cement, five hundred metres of timber and two thousand metres of wire fencing.'

This is typical Mechanic talk. Mechanics prefer working with facts and figures while distrusting intuition and guesswork. They like to make decisions based on objective analysis and logical deductions. Mechanics collect reliable information which they then carefully scrutinise before a choice is made.

To get your message across to Mechanics, include phrases such as: 'The facts of the matter are as follows . . .', 'the evidence strongly suggests . . .', 'a logical approach indicates that . . .', 'objectively we can see that . . .'

Motivators

Their overriding characteristic is enthusiasm, excitement and a love of change, novelty and variety. Stevie Bright is informing the sales team about a proposed conference, assuring them excitedly, 'It will be really exciting and rewarding. I went last year and it was truly fantastic, a wonderful opportunity to hear all the top speakers in selling. I found the insights I gained amazingly helpful!'

Motivators are lively, exciting people to be with, capable of generating enthusiasm and making people feel good about themselves, their work and their goals.

To get your message across to Motivators use words

which strike a chord with their love of the unusual, the unfamiliar and the unexpected: 'This is the most exciting idea I have heard in years . . .', 'I feel so enthused by this brilliant new project . . .', 'You'll love the novelty of this proposal.'

Why the Eyes Have It

If you watch closely while somebody is talking, you may notice something interesting about the way they move their eyes. At certain points in their conversation some people may glance up and to the right, while others look sideways left, or down to the right.

According to studies carried out by practitioners of Neuro-Linguistic Programming (NLP) these differences in eye movements are no mere chance occurrences. They reveal ways in which those individuals think about and respond to the world.

To understand and use NLP fully you need to be professionally trained in the technique. However, here is a taster of what can be gleaned by studying eye movements.

Visualisers

These are people who think mainly in pictures and images. They move their gaze up and to the left when recalling a factual event, such as describing their drive to work, but up and to the right when inventing something. Ask someone you think might be a Visualiser to imagine a purple elephant sky-diving into a giant bowl of custard, and notice whether the eyes move upward and to the right.

When communicating with a Visualiser use vivid word pictures and include words such as 'show', 'clear', 'see' and 'looking'. For example: 'Let me describe how the finished project will look. Imagine three tall, white marble

65

columns each carrying part of the slogan, standing against a clear blue background.'

Use phrases like: 'I see what you mean', 'I like the look of that', 'Let me show . . .', 'We have our target sight . . .'

Auditories

These are people who think mainly in terms of sounds and words. They move their eyes *sideways* and to the left when recalling events but sideways and to the right when inventing them.

As before you can check this with the sky-diving elephant image. If they look *down* and to the left they are engaged on an internal dialogue.

To get your message across to Auditories use phrases such as: 'I hear what you are saying', 'I like the sound of that', 'I'd like to tell you about my ideas . . .'

But if you see them look down and to the left, stop talking. It's a sign they are carefully reviewing what you have been saying by means of an internal dialogue.

Kinaesthetics

These people are very conscious of the way their own bodies are moving and responding. They often have excellent co-ordination and are highly sensitive to gestures, posture and expression in others. They look down and to the right when relaxed and down to the left when thinking.

To get your message across with them use phrases which include a notion of physical contact: 'I feel we are on the right lines', 'I sense this is the direction we should move in', 'I hold him in great respect', 'Let me touch on three key issues.'

Be sure to use effective body language when dealing with Kinaesthetics.

Although non-verbal communication is essential in all

forms of communication (see Chapter Twelve), it is especially important with this group of people.

In summary, to get your message across successfully you must start with an awareness of your audience's needs and then, so far as possible, match the content and delivery style to those needs.

Achieve awareness by positive listening, a skill which can only be perfected through regular practice. Listen to the way others use words and, in a one-to-one situation, match your delivery style to suit those preferred ways of communicating.

Only once this awareness has been achieved should you move to the second stage and consider how to structure the message in order to achieve your communication goals.

CHAPTER 4

Creating Magic Messages

A sub-dural haematoma was occasioned in the victim resulting from violent contact with a dynamic load impact device, this is a rapid-deceleration iterative inelastic-collision generator intended for short range ferrous cylinder bonding.

Extract from a medical report
Translator's note:
He was hit on the head with a hammer.

A few years ago I was attending the board meeting of a multinational company at which the directors received a report from the head of their computing department on proposals to upgrade their main frame. The man was an appalling communicator who spent 30 minutes alternately boring and bewildering an increasingly restless audience.

When he finally finished one of the directors asked whether his proposals would have a significant impact on the company's bottom line. This launched the boffin into a further ten minutes of jargon-filled ramblings.

He sat down amidst a perplexed silence, which was finally broken by the chairman, who commented in pained tones: 'I believe the word he was searching for was "Yes"!'

As I emphasised in earlier chapters, the first rule of successful communication is to speak to your audience in language it can understand. While this might seem like no more than simple common sense, time and again I have heard or read messages which either patronised or baffled the majority of those to whom they were directed.

You will only get your message across smoothly, successfully and effectively by avoiding:

- Messages which are overly complex, jargon-filled or pitched at a level of technical knowledge beyond the expertise of your audience;
- Language so simplistic it patronises the audience;
- Poor delivery when the message is spoken, i.e. your speech is too rapid and/or poorly enunciated or too quietly delivered for listeners to understand easily.

The secret of creating messages which move and motivate your listeners is to ensure they have built-in MAGIC. This acronym reminds us of the five elements crucial to effective and persuasive communications. The key words are:

M Motivating and Meaningful—to the audience for whom they are intended.

A Attention-grabbing: on most occasions you will only have a short time to capture anyone's interest and persuade them to see personal relevance in your message.

G Generate enthusiasm: while your ability to do this is often seen as owing more to your style of communication than it does to the content of your message, structure plays a vital role. Excitement has to be built into the fabric of your communication, in the words you use as well as in the way you use them.

I   Involve your audience: your ability to do this also depends not only on what you have to say, but how you say it and the excitement you generate. It is directly related to the WIIFM factor and depends on awareness of your audience's needs.

C   Content: the final letter brings us back to the first element. To be successful your communications must be both motivating and meaningful.

Let's explore each of these components in greater detail.

Creating Motivating Messages

We can be motivated towards something or away from something. Some people, for example, might decide to take up exercise not because they enjoy physical activity but in order to *avoid* putting on weight or getting out of condition. You might also be persuaded to install security equipment in your home to *prevent* a burglary.

A salesman who warned you that half the homes in your neighbourhood had been broken into over the past five years would be using a technique known as the 'fear sell' to motivate you to buy from him.

While messages urging people to avoid or prevent some negative outcome can be powerful and effective under the right circumstances, they also create some problems of communication.

Because they arouse the negative emotions of apprehension, anxiety or fear, they may trigger the powerful psychological defence mechanisms of denial or avoidance. In other words we switch off, by either refusing to think about the situation at all or denying its relevance to us.

As a result, messages which seek to motivate us away

from some action or situation often prove less successful than those which try and persuade us to do or achieve something.

There are 14 major human motivations. These are listed below but, apart from the first two which are generally held to be the most powerful motivators of all, they are not ranked in any particular order of importance.

- A desire for personal power and control over one's destiny
- Ego gratification—satisfying one's sense of self
- Emotional security
- Loving and being loved
- Self-esteem, dignity, self-respect
- The desire to win, to excel, to be the best
- A sense of belonging to some place or group
- Opportunities to be creative
- Accomplishing worthwhile goals
- Seeking out new experiences
- The enjoyment of freedom and privacy
- Social or peer group approval
- Recognition of one's efforts
- Financial security.

Everything we do in life is directed towards meeting these needs and we only ever feel truly fulfilled when each is adequately satisfied.

In order to get your message across you must ensure that you offer a means, or the promise of finding the means, by which your listener can accomplish one or more of these life goals.

Message Check List 1

Does my message help the listener achieve one or more of the fourteen key motivators?

Creating Meaningful Messages

It may appear obvious that, to get your message across successfully, it has to be readily understood by your audience. Unfortunately, as I explained above, people all too often forget the primary purpose of communication either through incompetence or from a desire to impress us with their knowledge and erudition.

How meaningful a particular message will be to your intended listeners depends on a variety of factors, especially their knowledge and experience of the subject.

Make your message too technical and you will leave many in your audience baffled. Pitch it at too low a level of expertise and you risk leaving an equal number feeling at best bored and at worst patronised. The only way to discover the right level of complexity for a particular message is by finding out all you can about your audience in advance.

Ask yourself: What do they need to know for my message to get across to them? What knowledge, experience and understanding do they have of the topic?

But always avoid:

Jargon: many professions, medicine, computing and the law among them, use words unknown to outsiders. Avoid these whenever possible if speaking to an audience unversed in that particular field.

Acronyms: some of these may be so widely used and so familiar in your area of expertise that it comes as a surprise to discover many people outside your business have little or no notion of what you mean.

72

Once you have lost your listeners on an unfamiliar acronym, one of two things is likely to happen. They will assume the message is beyond them and switch off, or miss several parts of your presentation as they puzzle about the unknown letters.

Message Check List 2

Is my message expressed in words which my listener can readily understand?

Creating Attention-Grabbing Messages

I shall discuss the importance of your opening remarks in the next chapter. But catching your listeners' attention within the first moments of starting to speak is essential if you are to hold their attention for the duration of the message.

A good opening not only makes them sit up and take notice, it also creates positive expectation about what will follow. A bad opening, by contrast, can send a silent— and sometimes not so silent—groan of disappointment around the room. Even if you then pick up speed and start attracting attention it may still be too late to win back all your listeners.

Message Check List 3

Are my opening words sufficiently attention-grabbing to make people want to listen to me?

Creating Enthusiasm-Generating Messages

The priceless ingredient in every effective presentation, enthusiasm is not the result but the cause of success. As Henry Ford said:

You can do anything if you have enthusiasm. Enthusiasm is the yeast that makes your hopes rise to the stars. Enthusiasm is the sparkle in your eye, it is the swing in your gait, the grip of your hand, the irresistible surge of your will and your energy to execute your ideas. Enthusiasts are fighters. They have fortitude. They have staying qualities. Enthusiasm is at the bottom of all progress! With it there is accomplishment. Without it there are only abilities.

Whatever the message you are getting across, enthusiasm is essential to persuade your audience to see things from your point of view. Without it you will appear uncertain, diffident, unconvinced or simply bored. By communicating enthusiasm through your words, voice tone and body language you will come across as energetic, inspiring and confident. But the starting point has to be a strong belief in the message you are communicating. Only the convinced can ever be truly convincing and only the persuaded are ever able to persuade.

Message Check List 4

Am I able to get this message across in a way which stimulates enthusiasm for my ideas or proposals?

Creating Involving Messages

You have to make people grasp the relevance of your message to them personally. Let them see clearly how your ideas will benefit their lives and they will be with you all the way. In part this is achieved through the use of language, in part by means of your non-verbal behaviour.

Message Check List 5

Have I constructed my message in such a way that it will generate a sense of personal involvement in my listeners?

Creating the Content of Your Message

The only way to achieve this is through a clear understanding of your audience's needs and this demands research. The more you know about your subject and the audience to whom you are speaking the more effective, persuasive and confident you will feel.

The secret of a successful communication can be summed up in just three words—research, research, research! You will find a list of research sources in the appendix.

Message Check List 6

Does my message reflect a satisfactory understanding of my listener's needs?

If you can honestly answer YES to each of these message check list questions, it is virtually certain that your message will not only get through to your intended audience but produce the desired results. As a final check on any message you are about to deliver, run it through the following BREAKFAST menu.

To create and deliver persuasive communications which succeed in getting your message across, you must always:

B Believe in the value and truth of your communication;
R Remember to take personality differences into account so that the way your message is delivered matches the communication needs of your audience;
E Evoke enthusiasm and generate excitement;

A Arouse interest and capture the attention;

K Knowledge—communicate it at a level appropriate to the expertise of your audience;

F Focus attention on the key issues by avoiding confusion or irrelevant details;

A Allow your listener(s) to achieve one or more of their motivational goals;

S Stimulate your audience to take the actions you expect and desire;

T Take account of the time available for you to communicate that information.

CHAPTER 5

Building a Structure for Success

Speech is a mirror of the soul: as a man speaks, so is he.
Publilius Syrus' Moral Sayings, first century BC

Bertrand Russell, the British philosopher and mathematician, once remarked that at least half the sins of mankind are caused by the fear of boredom. Certainly more than half the problems which arise when we try to communicate with one another results from the same problem. The moment people lose interest in your message they switch off and start thinking about something more rewarding.

You can beat the boredom barrier by:

- Ensuring your message is concisely structured and has a clear purpose;
- Delivering your message in a relaxed and conversational manner, whether you are chatting to one person or a thousand. I shall deal with ways of ensuring you achieve this relaxed, informal style of communicating in Chapter Ten.

For the moment, we'll focus on ways of beating the boredom barrier. To do this your message must have:

- A specific purpose
- A clear-cut structure
- Points which develop your ideas in a logical, consistent and meaningful way.

If you are preparing a written message, or writing a speech, talk or presentation you will later speak aloud, here's how to set about it.

THE MESSAGE MATRIX

Before starting to write, you may find it helpful to locate your proposed message in the matrix below. This relates the degree of formality expected to the level of seriousness involved, ranging from very formal and serious in the top left box to informal and not very serious in the lower right compartment.

SERIOUS AND FORMAL	FORMAL NOT SERIOUS
SERIOUS BUT INFORMAL	NOT SERIOUS OR FORMAL

Into the top left-hand box go messages for occasions which are both serious and formal, such as presenting a paper at an academic conference. People attending such meetings expect speakers to provide large amounts of information in a formal manner. This usually involves reading a printed speech (generally indifferently!) while standing behind a podium.

At top right are those occasions which, while having some formality about them, need not be taken entirely seriously. Sales and end of year company conferences often come into this category. Even though they are delivering important messages about their company's progress and performance, most speakers, from CEOs down, usually try to entertain, amuse and rally the troops as well as providing facts and figures.

The lower left box contains messages which, while serious in purpose, should be delivered in a less formal manner. Presenting your proposals at a company meeting or pitching for new business with prospective clients might slot in here.

Finally there are times when you deliver messages in a way which is both informal and not very serious. Even when you are communicating important information as part of the message, the emphasis is on being as entertaining as possible.

While there are obviously exceptions to these general rules, it is worth recognising right from the start which of these boxes your present communication is likely to fall into.

If you send confused signals, for instance by communicating a serious message in too informal a manner or talking about light-hearted issues in an overly formal way, your audience will feel confused and maybe even insulted by your style.

I should add that even when delivering a serious message in a formal setting, doing so in a relaxed and conversational manner will be tremendously helpful in getting your message across.

There is no need, as many speakers seem to believe, to communicate their messages in a manner which comes across, verbally and non-verbally, as stiff, aloof and remote. These days, probably as a result of television, most listeners want speakers to sound like human beings rather than automata.

One of President Reagan's greatest skills, and certainly

the reason why he was afforded the accolade of the 'great communicator', was that, unlike so many politicians, he talked *to* his listeners rather than *at* them.

At no time in his presidency was this more apparent than on 28 January, 1986, when he paid tribute to the crew who had just perished in the Challenger disaster. Although it was a tragic, serious and formal occasion, Reagan's tone remained conversational as he quoted the words which were to become famous: 'Oh I have slipped the surly bonds of Earth ... Put out my hand and touched the face of God.'[1]

This provides a classic example of a speech-writer, in this case Peggy Noonan, finding an appropriate quotation for the mood of the moment.

Once you are clear about the degree of formality and seriousness appropriate to the occasion, you are ready to start putting your thoughts down on paper.

Here are eight practical ways to get the creative juices flowing.

1   When producing the preliminary draft of your message, do not worry over much about getting the content 100 per cent correct the first time around. It is far better to allow your thoughts to flow freely onto the page or computer screen, even at the risk of some sloppy sentences or poorly constructed paragraphs. You will find it much easier to edit a text than to create, so leave any tidying up until you have written down all your ideas.

    If you have difficulty knowing where to begin, note down anything which comes to mind related to your

---

[1] This quotation, sometimes referred to as 'the pilot's creed', is from the sonnet 'High Flier', by Royal Canadian Air Force flyer Gillespie Magee. He died, aged 19, when his Spitfire crashed on 11 December, 1941.

message. Start by defining your objectives. Ask yourself:

- What do I want to achieve by getting my message across?
- What type of audience will I be communicating to?
- How much time will I have to communicate?
- How will I know if my message gets across?
- Is my purpose to inform, to persuade or to do both?

Jot down a series of headings, each with its set of related bullet points. This enables you to take in the overall structure of your message at a glance and warns if you start going off at a tangent.

More than six bullet points under a particular heading suggests you may be going into unnecessary detail. Avoid this by breaking that single heading into a number of items.

Restrict the content to the points your audience really needs to know in order to achieve your purpose.

Put yourself in your listeners' position by asking: 'If I was being given this message what would I want or need to hear?'

Once the basic structure has been created you can start on the message itself.

Write an introduction outlining your aims and briefly listing the topics you intend to cover. Next develop each of these topics in as few words as possible. Finally summarise the main body of your message point by point before listing your conclusions. Make certain these are clear and convincing.

This structure—sometimes expressed as 'tell them what you are going to tell them, tell them and then tell them what you told them'—is ideal for any messages which take ten minutes or longer to deliver. It aids your listeners' recall by taking advantage of two facets of human memory which I described in Chapter Two, the primacy and recency effects.

By 'telling them what you are going to tell them', you prepare your listeners' (readers') minds for the information to come. By 'telling them what you told them' at the end, you reinforce recollection of the key ideas in your message.

2 Maintaining a fast writing pace will help keep your creative juices flowing and ensure your words sound natural when you speak them aloud.

3 Once your ideas are flowing, never stop to re-read what you have written or you will almost certainly start making changes to the text there and then. This distracts you and inhibits your creativity.

4 If you get stuck at any time speak your thoughts aloud. This often removes idea blocks and produces a text which is easier to read aloud (see below).

5 Use the words 'You' and 'Yours' at the start of the presentation so that all your listeners can easily see what is 'in it for them', i.e. plug into WIIFM power.

6 You will capture and retain your audience's attention more easily by painting word pictures when emphasising the key ideas. This is done by using some of the rhetorical devices, especially analogy, simile, metaphor and triads, described in the next chapter.

7 Use positive, energising words and phrases which communicate confidence, purpose and action. The most powerful high-energy words you can include when your goal is to excite and stimulate your listener(s) are:

appreciate	assurance	confidence	convenience
courtesy	discover	dependable	easy
economy	efficient	enjoyment	expert
experienced	fun	genuine	growth

guarantee	health	help	love
modern	money	necessary	new
original	peace of mind	popular	pride
profitable	protection	prestige	quality
reputation	results	save	security
services	share	stimulating	stylish
successful	thank you	understand	unexcelled
you	your.		

Some of these words reflect deep feelings while others offer realistic and unbelievable solutions to problems, assurances of safety, security, fun and happiness.

But beware of words and phrases which possess plenty of energy but may come across as insincere or mere hype. These include: between you and me; brand new; Do you follow me?; fabulous; How are you?; out of this world; really; unbelievable; you ought; you should; you must!

Make certain every word employed works hard. In a short presentation you cannot carry passengers.

8   When revising your message, ruthlessly excise any words and phrases which add nothing to your message. Common examples of these time-wasting phrases include:

'It goes without saying . . .'—so why bother to say it?

'It's hardly necessary to repeat . . .'—so why take time repeating it?

'I would like to start by saying . . .'—just say it!

'A lot of time and effort has gone into this presentation . . .'—your audience is almost certainly interested only in the outcome, not the process by which your message was put together.

'I feel sure you will understand . . .'—never put money on it!

Also to be avoided are 'filler' remarks such as 'Which reminds me of a story . . .' and 'In conclusion . . .' These add nothing useful to the presentation and make it sound stilted and formal.

SIX TRAPS TO AVOID WHEN WRITING YOUR MESSAGE

Trap 1: Going on for Too Long

'Brevity is the soul of wit,' said Polonius, in Shakespeare's *Hamlet*.

It is also essential to getting your message across effectively. The most common trap into which inexperienced communicators fall is trying to cover too much ground. It is far better to restrict yourself to no more than three key points, which you will be able to communicate clearly and accurately, than to try to get across dozens of ideas none of which your audience properly takes on board.

As one US Congressman complained recently:

'The Lord's prayer is only 56 words long; Lincoln's Gettysburg Address is 268 words long; the Declaration of Independence is 1,322 words long; and the Federal Government's cabbage code, which regulates the sale of cabbages, is 26,911 words long.

People able to get their message across in the fewest possible well chosen words will be listened to more intently and enjoy greater respect as speakers than garrulous folk who take 30 minutes to communicate information which could just as easily have been conveyed in three.

BOX SIX

When Two High Flyers Were Grounded

Aviation pioneers Wilbur and Orville Wright must rank high among the world's most reluctant and briefest speakers. One day at a luncheon for a group of inventors, Wilbur was called upon to speak by the toastmaster. Rising unwillingly, he protested, 'There's been a mistake. Orville is the one who does all the talking.' The toastmaster turned to Orville, who rose briefly and said, 'Wilbur just made the speech.'

One of the masters of the pithy comment was Sir Winston Churchill who, called upon to make an impromptu speech about sex, stood up and announced: 'It gives me great pleasure,' before sitting down again amidst a storm of laughter and applause.

Follow the KISS strategy and Keep your message Simple and Straightforward, and know when to sit down and shut up. As all sales professionals are well aware, you can talk somebody out of doing something you want by carrying on for too long. Never forget that Samson slew 10,000 Philistines with the jawbone of an ass, and every day thousands of good ideas are killed in the same way!

Trap 2: Rambling Around the Point

This is caused by a lack of structure and cohesiveness. It is most likely to occur when people either try speaking off the cuff, or deviate from a prepared text. Avoid it through careful preparation and by keeping your mind fixed firmly on the reasons *why* you are communicating in the first place. Bear in mind the advice given by the King of Hearts in *Alice in Wonderland*: 'Begin at the beginning and go on till you come to the end: then stop.'

Trap 3: The Ink-Stained Text

This applies when you are preparing a talk or speech to be read aloud.

Writing for silent reading is very different from writing for speaking. Sentences which flow smoothly off the printed page when you are reading to yourself are liable to sound stilted when spoken. An 'easy listening' formula developed by broadcasting expert Irving E. Fang says: 'In any sentence, if the number of syllables minus the number of words is more than 20 it is too difficult to take in.' Experience suggests this may be overgenerous. Speak the following sentence out loud, score it according to the easy listening formula, and see whether you agree: 'Multisyllable utterances and subordinate clauses significantly and drastically reduce aural comprehensibility'.

Prevent 'ink staining' by always reading your script aloud into a tape recorder and listening carefully to how it sounds on playback.

Write for your own particular style of speech using sentence structures and words which flow easily from your lips. Never attempt to say anything that feels awkward or uncomfortable when you are reading it; rephrase the message until it can slip easily off your tongue. Beware, too, words and phrases you are uncertain about or have difficulty pronouncing.

You will achieve a relaxed conversational style more easily if you imagine you are talking to a friend instead of writing for strangers.

Trap 4: Straying off the Point

A message which starts by catching the audience's attention but then wanders into irrelevances betrays a speaker who is just trying to get by, or filling time. As with poor

---

BOX SEVEN

The Night I Insulted Royalty

When I first started in broadcasting, many years ago, I had to introduce a taped interview with a member of the royal family. In my script I included the fatal phrase 'he is renowned for being a shining wit'. On the night it came out completely differently, provoking complaints and leading to my temporary banishment from the microphone.

---

structure, this results from inadequate planning and shows a disrespect for the audience. Avoid this by developing the discipline of thinking about your presentation in a focused manner.

One useful exercise is to summarise the main points of your message in 50 words or less. This is the number which can be read in 20 seconds at a reasonable and easily understood rate of delivery. As a guide there are exactly 50 words in this fairly short paragraph.

Trap 5: Not Allowing Yourself Enough Time

Lack of time comes into two categories—preparation and presentation of the message

Preparation Time

Never attempt to prepare a complex message at the last moment. Allow yourself time to do any necessary research, to reflect on the main points you want to get across and to develop a logical structure through which to present and support those ideas. There may be some people who can scribble a keynote speech on the back of an envelope as they sit waiting to speak, but for most people working out what to say and how best to say it takes time.

There are, of course, techniques for thinking on your feet and dealing with unexpected objections, which I shall be describing in Chapter Eight. But the main part of your message almost always has to be planned and thought through well before the moment you open your mouth to speak. For most of us, speaking without thinking is like shooting without aiming. Your chances of hitting the right target are slim indeed.

Presentation Time

Make certain your message can be got across in the time available without compelling you to rush through the final points.

A complicated message takes longer to deliver in practice than it does when you rehearse, usually by around 25 per cent. This means a speech lasting 12 minutes during rehearsal will require 15 minutes on the day.

How long should a speech last? There seems to be a consensus among professional speakers and speech-writers that 20 minutes—approximately the normal span of human attention—plus ten minutes for questions and answers is a good average benchmark.

The 20-minute period should comprise:

General introduction (2–3 minutes). As I have already explained, this must grab your audience's attention, establish your credibility, create some goodwill and preview the body of the speech.

This is a tough challenge but one you can meet, providing you avoid rambling, miss out irrelevant comments and get right down to the point.

Here's a sample of how to do it from Clive Chajet,

chairman, Lippincott & Margulies Inc, in a keynote address at the Conference Board's Conference on 'Energising Performance with Communication':

> The question before us is ... how can communications break down the barriers to improved corporate performance?
>
> Before I start swinging wildly at this very broad issue, I want to narrow the subject to five barriers that are both important and vulnerable. Important in their impact on an organisation. And vulnerable in that attacking them in the right ways with the right communications tools will make a difference.
>
> Before I take them on one at a time ... let's look at them as a group.
>
> They are:
>
> - The barrier of perception versus reality.
> - The barrier of home-grown misconceptions.
> - The barrier of provincial constraints.
> - The barrier of initial resistance.
> - And in some ways the most difficult of all, the barrier of short-sighted disinterest.[1]

Notice how this speaker gains attention by asking a question, and then creates an interest among his audience by previewing the topic with repetition of the word 'barrier'.

As I explain in the next chapter, repetition is a powerful and ancient rhetorical device which can greatly assist you in getting your own messages across.

If you want to start with a joke or an anecdote by all means do so (see Chapter Ten), but make certain it is

1 Clive Chajet, 'Breaking Down Image Barriers', delivered in Los Angeles, California, 30 September, 1994. Quoted in *The Executive Speaker Newsletter*, vol. 16, no. 1, January 1995.

relevant to your topic and helps to create the right atmosphere for your message.

Body of the Message (14–16 minutes).
Conclusions (2–3 minutes). As I explained above, this should restate the main points of your speech and focus on the response you desire from your audience.

A good conclusion should leave your listeners with a clear idea of the purpose behind your message and what they can, or should, do next.

Trap 6: Insufficient Supporting Information

An effective message should be like an iceberg, with far more below the surface than is visible to the naked eye. Whenever possible, gather three or four times as much information as you actually need to support each key point. Having a strong grasp of your subject helps you in three ways:

- It increases confidence and reduces anxiety.
- It enables you to 'think on your feet' more easily and makes it less likely you will be faced with a point on which you have no knowledge.
- It makes it less likely that you will forget key points in your message.

Knowledge of your audience, achieved through research, plays a major role in deciding the type and amount of supporting material required. Before deciding to include such information ask yourself:

- Is it relevant?
- Is it accurate?
- Is it reliable?
- Is it recent?
- Is it fairly stated?

90

- Is it typical?
- Is it appropriate and meaningful to my audience?

The supporting material should only be used if it meets all these qualifications.

ONE FINAL CHECK

Before delivering your message, check you have answers to the following questions:

WHAT am I going to communicate?
Make certain you fully understand your material and have thought through your conclusions which must be logical and well supported by the evidence.

WHY am I trying to get this message across?
What is your purpose and goal? How will you know whether this purpose has been achieved?

Is your message sufficiently important and compelling to take those attending away from their normal work?

WHO will be listening to me?
Reflect on your intended audience, whether this is one person or a thousand. Check that your choice of words matches their expectations and experience.

When talking to a large group of people you must never patronise the majority by aiming for the lowest common denominator. At the same time there is no point in delivering a message which only a minority present will understand.

The most effective and successful communicators have the ability to put across complex messages in a way which is understood by most, if not all, members of their audience.

HOW many people will I be communicating with?
The size of your audience will influence your style of presentation. With a smaller group, the approach can be more interactive and less formal than with a larger audience.

Now run through this six-point check list:

1   Is the structure logical? Does it have a beginning, a middle and end?
2   Have I prepared it in such a way that the delivery will be smooth, and comfortable?
    Have I avoided any words or phrases which will be hard to say (especially under the emotional pressure of communicating with a large audience) or difficult to understand?
3   Are my proposals supported by accurate facts and figures?
4   Will my audience understand all the terms used? Be especially careful about acronyms, technical words, jargon and phrases in a foreign language.
5   Is every word in my message used correctly and precisely?
6   Does my message build to a clear and memorable conclusion?

Practise the points described in this chapter either by analysing a message which you recently delivered or by preparing one especially for this exercise. Remember every word used must work for you. There is no room for redundancy.

With an important message, such as a speech you are preparing to deliver at a conference, rehearse in front of a small audience who will provide objective and honest feedback. Try to choose people who have background knowledge similar to that of your intended audience. Be sufficiently open-minded to take any criticisms seriously and make changes to your text where necessary.

CHAPTER 6

Putting Words to Work

Broadly speaking, the short words are the best, and the old words best of all.

Sir Winston Churchill

Rhetoric, defined by the *Oxford English Dictionary* as 'the art of using language so as to persuade or influence others', was first developed by the Greeks and Romans with an entirely practical purpose in mind.

Because the Greeks had no lawyers (pause here to marvel at their common sense), Athenian citizens who wanted to sue or were being sued had to make their own case before a jury of fellow citizens, a jury which, on occasions, numbered as many as 1,500. The more eloquently they spoke the more likely they were to persuade fellow citizens of the justness of their cause and win their case.

Being a skilled public speaker was also essential to those ambitious for power, since leadership of the Athenian

Assembly depended almost entirely on their persuasive powers. Pericles (490–429 BC), who gave his name to an age, achieved and retained power not via the ballot box but by means of superior debating skills.

The fact that some speakers were so much more successful than others aroused the curiosity of some Greeks who set out to discover what made them such powerful orators. They quickly established that the *way* in which a message was delivered was just as important, frequently even more so, than *what* was said.

This discovery led to the world's earliest ghost-writers, men like the famous Greek orator Lysias (c.458–c.380 BC) and Antiphon of Rhamnus (430–411 BC), who used their skills not only to provide a 'voice' for less gifted speakers but also to coach them in the most effective ways of delivering those lines.

One who carefully studied and followed the rhetorical techniques pioneered by the Greeks and Romans was William Shakespeare. Not only was he one of the world's greatest playwrights, he was also an accomplished speech-writer, who penned 31,959 of them in his 37 plays.

An actor himself, Shakespeare wrote more for the ear than the eye, choosing words which had the power to move his audiences to laughter, anger, fear or sorrow.

In *Julius Caesar*, Shakespeare describes the six traits he believed every effective orator must possess. Following the assassination of Caesar, Mark Antony explains to the crowd that he is no orator, but a 'plain, blunt man' who lacks the skills needed to sway people by eloquence:

> For I have neither wit, nor words, nor worth,
> Action, nor utterance, nor power of speech
> To stir men's blood

In Shakespeare's day *wit*, his first quality, meant wisdom or intelligence. *Words* refers to the choice and use of vocabulary, while his third quality, *worth*, means the speaker's character and reputation.

Action denotes gesture and expression, what today we would call the non-verbal aspects of delivering a message. The fifth quality, *utterance*, means the words must be enunciated clearly and accurately. His final quality, *the power of speech*, refers to the presentational style, the manner in which the speaker gets his or her message across.

You may feel that rhetoric and oratory have little to do with the type of messages you have to deliver, one to one across your desk, during meetings, in the board room or at conferences. But the truth is that present-day speakers ignore the ancient rules of rhetoric at their peril. These are no historical relics but potent stylistic devices employed by great speakers and writers down the centuries. They are still as valid and effective today as they were more than 2,000 years ago.

By employing them yourself you will get your message across in a far more compelling and convincing manner.

Rhetorical devices fall into two main categories:

- Figures of speech.
- Figures of structure.

FIGURES OF SPEECH

The three most widely used are:

- Similes
- Metaphors
- Analogies.

Similes

These are used to make comparisons between different things, by stating that something is 'like' or 'as' something else. In *The Winter's Tale*, for example, Shakespeare uses a simile to compare a hand with the texture and colour of a bird's feathers: 'As soft as dove's down and as white.'

And here's how one present-day speaker used the same device to add a touch of humour to his message:

> Being a regulator these days is a lot like being the nearest fire hydrant to the dog pound. You know they'll have to turn to you in an emergency . . . but it's sure tough dealing with those daily indignities.[1]

Metaphors

These imply that two different things *are* similar, by describing one thing in terms of another—as when Macbeth says that 'Life's but a walking shadow'.

A more complex metaphor occurs at the start of *Richard III* which opens with the line: 'Now is the winter of our discontent'. By combining 'winter' and 'discontent' Shakespeare suggests that just as 'winter' is the coldest season of the year, so is 'discontent' the coldest season of the emotions.

The metaphor is an especially powerful rhetorical device since it helps an audience unfamiliar with your area of expertise to understand your arguments through reference to something that they do know about. Here's how American Medical Association executive vice-president Dr

1 Eugene A. Ludwig, Office of the Comptroller of the Currency, Remarks on Federal Regulatory Reform, delivered at the Town Hall of Los Angeles, California, 24 July, 1995.

James Todd used a theatrical metaphor to explain his concerns over insurance industry policies:

> I think of health system reform as a three-act play.
>
> Act I is over already. It involved a lot of sound and fury, signifying nothing more than a stormy beginning.
>
> Now the curtain is up on Act II, and all you have to do is turn on the nightly news to see the level of confusion and diversity that now exists. Everyone is trying to rewrite the script, and I have a feeling there's going to be a lot of blood on the stage before this act is over later this year.
>
> The big finale—Act III—is yet to come. That's when health system reform changes how medicine in this country will be practised well into the next century. So the stage is set, and the real action has begun.[1]

Although similes and metaphors normally emphasise just one similarity between the things being compared, they can on occasions be combined for even greater effect, as in this passage from *Twelfth Night*:

> If music be the food of love, play on;
> . . .
> O! it came o'er my ear like the sweet sound
> That breathes upon a bank of violets . . .

1 James S. Todd MD, 'The Challenge of Change: Ensuring the Public Interest', delivered at Health Insurance Association of America, Washington DC, 3 May, 1994. Quoted in *The Executive Speaker Newsletter*, vol. 15, no. 9, September 1994.

Analogies

These describe similarities between things, as in *Henry V*, where Shakespeare constructs an entire speech on the idea that divisions of function, authority and responsibility can be found in all organised communities.

> Therefore doth heaven divide
> The state of man in divers functions,
> Setting endeavour in continual motion,
> To which is fixed as an aim or butt
> Obedience. For so work the honey-bees,
> Creatures that by a rule in nature teach
> The act of order to a peopled kingdom.

Likening the society of bees, point by point, to human society, enables him to demonstrate that they share many similarities.

By comparing the unfamiliar with the familiar, an analogy helps your listeners make sense of what might otherwise strike them as strange ideas.

In this speech extract, by Roger Roberts, a vice-president at the McDonnell Douglas Corporation, a comparison is drawn between the need for inspired partnership in the aerospace industry and the teamwork which helped space scientists meet the challenge of the Apollo 13 crisis:

A few minutes after Jim Lovell and his fellow astro-nauts signed off from their . . . telecast, they heard a loud bang. One of the two oxygen tanks in the rear service module had exploded. Warning lights glowed red in the cockpit from the looming shutdown on life-support systems. At the same time, the spacecraft began to rock and tumble as gas vented from the one remaining oxygen tank.

What made the Apollo 13 mission memorable was an amazing recovery from a lethal set of circumstances. Like the British evacuation from Dunkirk in World War II, Apollo 13 is an example of inspired team-work and creativity in a narrow escape from disaster . . .

Once again, I believe that we are in a tight situation which calls for something extra from all of us.

In the present circumstances, we are not faced with the searing immediacy of an Apollo 13-type crisis. But we are faced with a crisis nonetheless. There has been a major shutdown in some life-support systems backing US dominance in military and civilian space.[1]

When preparing your messages, make use of these three figures of speech, the simile, metaphor and analogy, to add greater clarity, comprehension and power to your ideas.

FIGURES OF STRUCTURE

Alliteration

This technique of linking words starting with the same sound or letter can prove very effective when used in moderation, as in this passage from Tennyson's *The Princess* which contains several groups of alliterative words:

The splendour falls on castle walls
  And snowy summits old in story:
The long light shakes across the lakes,
  And the wild cataract leaps in glory.

1 Roger Roberts, 'Apollo 13: Lessons for Going Forward in Space', delivered at Armed Forces Communications and Electronics Association, Colorado Springs, Colorado, 12 August, 1955. Quoted in *The Executive Speaker Newsletter*, vol. 16, no. 10, October 1995.

Blow, bugle, blow, set the wild echoes flying,
Blow, bugle; answer, echoes, dying, dying, dying.

Alliteration enables you to emphasise certain words and create a rhythm which catches your audience's attention and intensifies the power of your message. But beware of using it too often or for too long since it can quickly become a predictable gimmick which starts to undermine the seriousness and diminish the strength of your message.

Epistrophe

This adds emphasis to your message by repeating the same word or phrases at the *end* of successive clauses. Since this is what your listeners hear last it can also be used to improve their recall of the passage through the recency effect, which I described earlier. Here is an example from Mark Antony's funeral speech in *Julius Caesar*:

For Brutus is an honourable man;
So are they all, all honourable men . . .
Ambition should be made of sterner stuff:
Yet Brutus says he was ambitious;
And Brutus is an honourable man . . .
Yet Brutus says he was ambitious:
And, sure, he is an honourable man.

Rhetorical Questions

These are questions raised in order to emphasise points you want to make rather than in expectation of answers. Shylock made use of this device when, in *The Merchant of Venice*, he demanded:

Hath not a Jew eyes? hath not a Jew hands, organs, dimensions, senses, affections, passions? . . . If you prick us, do we not bleed? if you tickle us, do we not laugh? if you poison us, do we not die? and if you wrong us, shall we not revenge?

By directly involving members of an audience in your message, and by compelling them to consider its details, rhetorical questions allow you to catch and hold their attention. Here's an extract from a speech by John J. McGrath, director of marketing and management communications for Argonne National Laboratory, which well illustrates this technique.

After commenting that, like doctors and lawyers, engineers seemingly shed their 'ability to speak common English in order to be licensed to practice', he continued:

> The same might be said for CEOs. True, most CEOs earned their positions. True, they tend to be fairly bright and fairly decisive. But in public, well . . .
> OK, so what?
> Why should we care? Why should CEOs care? If they turn a respectable profit, so what if they aren't especially charming and persuasive at Rotary Club meetings.[1]

Triads: The Power of Three

'Inanimate objects are classified scientifically into three major categories: those that don't work, those that break down, and those that get lost.' *New York Times* columnist Russell Baker's humorous comment introduces one of the

1 John J. McGrath, 'Sell Your CEO! Winning the Corporate-Image Battle in the 90s,' delivered at Communications Corridor Group, Chicago, Illinois, 21 March, 1995. Quoted in *The Executive Speaker Newsletter*, vol. 16, no. 7, July 1995.

most widely used and powerful of all rhetorical devices—
the triad.

By introducing the power of three into your communications you will be able to:

- Introduce emphasis and dramatic effect;
- Make your key points more memorable and easily
  recalled;
- Convey important ideas more clearly by breaking
  lengthy chunks of text into smaller, more easily understood units.

The triad involves grouping three words, phrases or
clauses as in 'Hip, hip, hooray', 'Ready, steady, go . . .'
'On and on and on' or 'Hello, hello, hello.'

Listing items together in this way will allow you to
strengthen, underline or amplify any kind of message from
the simplest to the most complex.

A famous triad known to every American child occurs
in Abraham Lincoln's Gettysburg Address: 'government
of the people, by the people, and for the people'.[1] But
although it has resonated through modern American history, Lincoln's noble sentiments were far from original.

Thirteen years earlier, the American Unitarian clergy-
man Theodore Parker had described a democracy as 'a
government of all the people, by all the people, for all the
people'.[2]

Twenty years before that, a speech by the American
lawyer and statesman Daniel Webster included the words:
'The people's government, made for the people, made by
the people, and answerable to the people.'[3]

Not that Webster could claim to the originator of this

1 19 November, 1863.
2 *The American Idea*, 29 May, 1850.
3 Second Speech on Foote's Resolution, 26 January, 1830.

thought. Four years previously, *Vivian Grey*, a first novel by the future prime minister of Great Britain, Benjamin Disraeli, included the sentence: '. . . all power is a trust—that we are accountable for its exercise—that, from the people, and for the people, all springs, and all must exist.'

Yet even Disraeli's comment was hardly original. Five centuries earlier, the English preacher John Wycliffe used an almost identical phrase: 'This Bible is for the government of the People, by the People, and for the People.' (Attributed, 1382)

By listing the above examples I am not trying to diminish the potency of the message each of these very different speakers sought to convey, but to illustrate the fact that the power of three has, for centuries, been recognised by professional communicators.

Many sophisticated examples of triads occur in Shakespeare, as for instance this extract from *Macbeth*:

> Life's but a walking shadow, a poor player,
> That struts and frets his hour upon the stage,
> And then is heard no more; it is a tale
> Told by an idiot, full of sound and fury,
> Signifying nothing.

Notice how Shakespeare has expressed his character's weariness and dissatisfaction with life by means of a powerful triple metaphor. Macbeth views his existence as being no more substantial than a shadow; as brief as an actor's performance; and as meaningless as the chattering of a fool.

While triads are a powerful way of ending your message, they are equally effective any time you want to emphasise key parts of a communication, as this speech by W. H. Chrome George, former Chairman of the Aluminum Company of America, demonstrates:

Technology is not, science is not, certainly management is not the enemy of old values, old heritages or old cultures.

Since the most primitive times, for example, simple technology has served as a sustaining force for the cultures which have survived for centuries.

The spear, the net, the plough, the loom and many other such technologies served to give the ancient cultures their surviving strength. Today's technology—liberating the human spirit from the oppression of ancient labours—is servant, not master, of our enduring beliefs. With patience, with understanding, but with persistence and courage, managers must function on the leading edge to allay the fears, overcome the misconceptions and answer the mindless misrepresentations about what orderly progress may bring.[1]

Combining triad and paired elements can also create a powerful effect, as is shown in this extract from a speech given by Howard M. Love of National Steel Corp. at the Economic Club of Detroit: 'But it will take sacrifice; it will take forbearance; and, it will certainly take a consistent concern for productivity and investment. In short, it will take action, not words.'

If you do not already do so, start using triads in your messages right away. You will be astonished how much more successfully you will be able to communicate ideas and motivate your listeners.

1 Quoted in Robert O. Skovgard, 'Figures of Sound', *National Underwriter*, 15 January 1983.

Contrastive Pairs

When, during the UK General Election in 1979, James Callaghan said: 'In this election I don't intend to *make* the most promises ... I intend that the next Labour government shall *keep* the most promises' he was using a rhetorical device called the contrastive pair.

These help you to get your message across when completing a point or delivering a punch line. If presented in the form of a puzzle they enable you to arouse your audience's curiosity.

During his morale-boosting speeches in World War II, Winston Churchill often used contrastive pairs and triads to spellbinding effect, as when he said: 'This is not the end. It is not even the beginning of the end. But it is, perhaps, the end of the beginning.'[1]

In the closing paragraphs of his inaugural address, President Kennedy used contrastive pairs when he exhorted his audience: 'ask not what your country can do for you— ask what you can do for your country.'[2]

Introduce contrastive pairs into your message by using any of the following five connector phrases which enable you to link two ideas together.

1 This ... not that.
   Example: 'Today's technology ... is servant, not master, of our enduring beliefs.'[3]
2 Because this ... then that.
   Example: 'America is great because America is good.'[4]
3 If this ... then that.

1 Mansion House speech, 10 November, 1942.
2 20 January, 1961.
3 W. H. Chrome George, quoted above, p. 105.
4 Alexis de Tocqueville.

106

Example: 'If a nation values anything more than freedom, it will lose its freedom.'[1]

4   Not this . . . but that.

Example: 'Not by speech making and the decisions of majorities will the questions of the day be settled . . . but by iron and blood.'[2]

5   From this . . . to that.

Example: 'I pass with relief from the tossing sea of Cause and Theory to the firm ground of Result and Fact.'[3]

Repetition

As I explained in a previous chapter, repeating a keyword, a key phrase or a structure will help you drive home our key point.

The effect is enhanced still further when combined with an element of suspense, as in this opening to a speech by G. Robert Truex Jr of Rainier Banking Corporation:

It has been an evil force: it has ravaged the lives of the poor; it has forced middle-income families into tax brackets intended for the wealthy; it has made fools out of savers; it has turned long-term, fixed-rate loans into long-term, fixed-rate losses; it has, in short, drained much of the lifeblood out of the American economy.

Notice also the powerful effect you can create by repeated use of the same sentence structure in this extract from remarks on voluntarism and philanthropy by William A. Andres when he was with Dayton Hudson Corporation:

1   W. Somerset Maugham.
2   Prince Otto von Bismarck.
3   Winston Churchill.

Could it be that some of the problems currently beset-
ting some of this country's major industries (industries now suffering decline); *could it be* that some of
these problems might have been lessened, had their
managements been more involved in their communities, more sensitive to changes in society and more
responsive to those changes?

Could some of the unsuccessful efforts to manage
change be traced to lack of attention to broader issues,
a lack of involvement in addressing the needs of
society as a whole, rather than just the business?

Might not many of these changes have been more
apparent to management, and management better
able to respond, had there been more corporate
involvement?

More voluntarism, more philanthropy, more strategic planning with an eye toward the changing con-
sumer, and more targeting of corporate resources into
solving problems that affect the total society, and thus
business?

Based on our experiences at Dayton Hudson, we
think the answer to those questions is an unqualified
'yes'.[1]

Mixed Sentence Length

Following a series of longer sentences with shorter ones
or fragments of sentences will allow you to create dramatic
effects.

Here is an example from the speech by William S.
Anderson of the NCR Corp.:

1 William A. Andres, Remarks on Voluntarism and Philanthropy, delivered
at Columbia University, New York City, 27 October, 1982, on the acceptance of the Lawrence A. Wein Prize in Corporate Responsibility.

As economist Lester Thurow has pointed out, the US economy today is bleeding from a 'thousand cuts.' I wish it were possible to say that business is blameless in this multiple, persistent wounding of the economy. But such is not the case.

Putting Them All Together

This extract from a speech by Shoichi Akazawa of Fujitsu Limited illustrates several of the stylistic devices described above in action. In addition he uses other techniques to put his message across in a forceful manner. After reading it, test your rhetorical skills by analysing the speech in terms of the style and structure devices described above.

I am afraid I must view the new decade as one of uncertainty, instability, and complexity for my country. I say this sadly.

One problem is our shortage of resources: to give two examples, 89% of our energy and 55% of our food come from abroad.

Another problem is the difficulty we have been having with various countries in matters of trade.

Still another is that our country is now beginning to suffer from what I shall call 'advanced nation disease.'

This illness, which has reached epidemic levels in some countries, is characterized by a loss of vitality on the part of the people, a drop in human energy, in drive to get things done.

In other words, we Japanese seem to lack '*busido seishin*', which means a strong sense of duty and loyalty. This malady is affecting Japan just as it is affecting various other countries.[1]

1 Mr Akazawa's speech appeared in *The Executive Speaker Newsletter*, vol. 2, no. 4, March 1981.

In this short extract Shoichi Akazawa uses four main rhetorical devices:

1   The rule of three several times, mainly in order to knit paragraphs together: 'Uncertainty, instability, and complexity'; 'One problem . . . Another problem . . . Still another'; 'A loss of vitality, a drop in energy, in drive'.

2   Changes in sentence length. A short sentence following the initial assertion adds a sense of drama: 'I say this sadly.'

3   A vivid metaphor: 'advanced nation disease' is then reinforced by use of the words 'illness', 'epidemic', and 'malady'.

4   A paired construction is used to draw a conclusion: 'This malady is affecting Japan just as it is affecting various other countries.'

How many did you identify?

Score 4: Excellent. You clearly have a sound grasp of rhetorical devices. Be sure to use them when getting important messages across.

Score 3: Good. You have a reasonable grasp of how some of the most powerful verbal presentation techniques identified can be used.

Score 2: Fair. Start using these persuasive techniques more frequently and you will quickly discover how helpful they prove.

Score 0–1: I suggest you review this chapter in order to get a better understanding of the many ways in which written and spoken messages can be communicated more successfully.

Do not be afraid of using the powerful rhetorical devices described in this chapter to add colour, interest and persuasiveness to your key messages. You will be amazed at how much they enhance your ability to communicate your ideas to the widest possible range of audiences.

Reject the leaden language which goes to make up the uninspired and uninspiring speeches trotted out by so many public speakers. As G. K. Chesterton remarked almost a century ago: 'The heavy and cautious responsibility of speech is the easiest thing in the world; anybody can do it. That is why so many tired, elderly, and wealthy men go in for politics!'[1] His gloomy words have as much truth and resonance today as they did at the turn of the century.

But while many modern politicians and bureaucrats would undoubtedly feel at ease with the rhetorical styles fashionable in the early 1900s, very few present-day audiences would tolerate them.

Today's listeners, raised in the fast-paced visual world of television, expect—or at least hope—to be communicated to in a similarly entertaining manner.

---

1 G. K. Chesterton, 'The Case for the Ephemeral', *All Things Considered*, 1908.

111

CHAPTER 7

Training and Using Your Voice

Who hath given man speech? or who hath set therein, a
snare for peril and a thorn for sin. For in the word his life
is and his breath, And in the word his death.
                    Algernon Swinburne, *Atalanta in Calydon*

It is ironic that while human beings have evolved areas of
the brain specialised for speech, and although it is our
ability to speak—what linguist Stephen Pinker calls 'the
language instinct'—which distinguishes us most pro-
foundly from other primates, we have no mechanisms
designed exclusively to enable us to speak.

The vocal folds, which vibrate in order to produce
sounds, were designed to stop food going down the wind-
pipe rather than the oesophagus. The main purpose of our
lungs, which provide the wind power with which to vibrate
the vocal cords, is to exchange gases, putting oxygen
into the body and expelling carbon dioxide. The reason
we have hollow spaces in the face bones—the sinuses—

which help us amplify sounds, is to make them lighter.

But although the equipment used to produce speech may have been cobbled together from bits and pieces originally intended for different purposes, this in no way diminishes its social and personal importance.

Poor delivery, which makes it hard either to hear or, having heard, to understand what a speaker is trying to say, is one of the most common complaints levelled by audiences. The six most frequently encountered speech barriers to getting one's message across are:

1   Speaking too softly. Even when those at the back can just about hear a low-volume speaker, it is tiring for them. Audiences have to work far harder to get the message and, unless it is of riveting importance to them, may quickly give up the struggle. Even when they are sufficiently interested or patient to listen to the whole message, the likelihood of misunderstandings clearly soars.

   Speaking too softly is often caused by a mixture of anxiety and poor breath control.

2   Swallowing words. Many people allow their voices to fall away at the end of the sentence, making it harder for audiences to hear every word. As with too quiet a delivery, word swallowing increases the risk of errors.

3   Running out of breath. Speakers who fail to breathe correctly run the risk of finding themselves breathless just at the moment when they want to emphasise a particular word or phrase. Instead of coming across with the impact intended, that key part of the message is lost to their audience.

4   Audible pause. This involves the meaningless 'umms' and 'ers' I discussed earlier. It also includes the habit of using words which add nothing to the message, such as 'well', 'you know' and 'see what I mean'.

113

Audible pauses are partly a matter of habit, partly a result of being afraid of silence, which is an element of speaker anxiety. When nervous we rush to fill silences with any sound, however unnecessary, inappropriate or meaningless.

The pause is one of the most dynamic speaking tools. Practise until you feel comfortable saying nothing in front of an audience for up to four seconds. Although, at first, you may start to panic, thinking the silence has lasted for ever, to your audience it will not only seem perfectly natural, but add extra punch to your message.

Use pauses to gain thinking time, to emphasise or dramatise key parts of your message, and to allow your listeners to gather their thoughts and reflect on what you have just said.

5   Speaking too rapidly. While it is important to speak at a pace which conveys energy and enthusiasm for the message, gabbling the words out, perhaps in order to escape from the ordeal as quickly as possible, makes it far harder for an audience to follow the message. By encouraging shallow breathing, rapid speech also increases anxiety.

Be prepared to change pace, just as you would gears on a car, to take account of different aspects of your speech.

While you might want to speed up slightly when recounting an anecdote or painting a word picture, it is advisable to slow right down and use more pauses when dealing with more complex messages. Incidentally, to ensure understanding and recall of these messages, be sure to provide some kind of visual support, either in the form of slides, overhead projection fiches or hand-outs. The importance of visual aids in clarifying your communications is discussed in Chapter Eleven.

6   Unvarying voice tone. There are few things on earth
    more conducive to sleep than a flat, monotonous, style
    of presentation.
        Avoid this trap by rehearsing key messages in front
    of the tape recorder and listening objectively to the way
    you come across. Making a tape recording is important
    since you never hear exactly how your voice sounds
    to others owing to distortions caused by the vibrations
    of bones in your skull.
        Put variety into your voice by varying the speed,
    pitch and volume of delivery. Remember that an
    unvarying drone makes it almost impossible for your
    audience to attend.
        Try to lower the register of your voice slightly,
    especially if it is normally rather light, since a deeper
    tone communicates greater authority and self-
    confidence.
        Slow down and drop your voice to signal that you
    are about to make a point of great interest and impor-
    tance. Pause and make eye contact with key members
    of the audience.

Marking Your Script

When reading from a prepared text, you may find it helpful
to write on the script using a notation which indicates how
those words are to be delivered. These marks tell you when
to pause, and for how long, when to slow down and when
to speed up, which words to emphasise and where it would
help to speak more loudly or more softly. Here's one type
of notation used by many professional speakers:

	Voice rises
	Voice falls
>	Speak louder
<	Speak more softly

———— Emphasise this point
// Long pause
/ Short pause
– Tie phrases for smoother flow.

BREATHING AND SPEAKING

We breathe between 16,000 and 20,000 times a day, and since breathing correctly is essential for speaking correctly, it will be useful to consider some of the different ways it can take place.

Some 3,000 years ago mystics claimed that 'life is in the breath', by which they meant far more than just lungs, blood, circulation and the exchange of gases. They meant that form of life energy the ancient Indian language of Sanskrit calls *prana*. Breath is the vehicle for *prana*.

When your breathing is inefficient this life force is diminished and anxiety rises.

When your breathing is full and efficient your whole system is enhanced, emotionally, physically and intellectually, which is why we describe somebody filled with creative life energy as being 'inspired' or having an 'inspiration'.

The Mechanics of Breathing

We can breathe in one of two main ways. The first is by raising the chest wall using intercostal muscles, attached between each rib. The second method is to flatten and contract the diaphragm, a strong, dome-shaped sheet of muscle separating the chest cavity and abdomen, while moving the upper ribs and breastbone forwards and upwards to increase chest capacity. In each case a partial vacuum is created in the chest cavity, drawing air into the lungs.

116

If your ribcage moves mainly outwards and upwards, your breathing is shallow and costal. If most of the work is done by your diaphragm and muscles forming the abdominal wall, your breathing is deep and diaphragmatic.

Diaphragmatic or abdominal breathing is by far the more efficient since expansion and ventilation occur in the lower parts of the lung which are richest in blood.

We breathe in this way when calm and composed. Diaphragmatic breathing itself helps generate a calm, composed, emotional state.

Exploring Your Breathing Machinery

Place the fingers of both hands along the lower edge of your ribs, beginning in the middle where they meet at the breastbone or sternum. Applying gentle pressure with your fingertips, distinguish the firmness of the ribcage from the softness of the abdomen. Follow the ribs towards your spine. At your back, the ribs are more difficult to detect owing to strong bands of muscles, so you will need to apply firmer pressure.

The diaphragm is anchored by a sheet of non-contractile tissue at the centre, to the lower ribs at the edges and to the upper lumbar vertebrae at the back.

Three crucial structures, the oesophagus, inferior vena cava and aorta, pass through the diaphragm, giving it an important role in digestion and circulation. It prevents acidic stomach juices passing back into the oesophagus and causing heartburn, and plays a role in returning blood to the heart from the legs, abdomen and pelvis.

The flattening and contracting action of the diaphragm increases abdominal pressure and this, together with the abdominal muscles, creates an inflatable jacket providing support to the lower back.

As the diaphragm contracts and flattens the volume of

the chest cavity increases, pulling air into the lungs via the nose or mouth. Chest size is also increased as the scalene muscles lift the upper ribs and breastbone forwards and upwards. The intercostal muscles, which are attached between each of the ribs, control the outward movement of the lower ribs.

Costal (of the ribs) or chest breathing is characterised by an outward and upward movement of the ribcage. Because chest expansion occurs at the midpoint, the middle of each lung gets most air. This is a less effective way of breathing since the lower parts of the lungs are richest in blood and therefore exchange gases most efficiently. It means your body has to do more work to achieve the same amount of blood gas mixing. The harder it works the more oxygen is required and the more breaths you have to take.

While costal breathing is helpful during brisk exercise it is inappropriate for everyday activities and, especially, for speaking in public. Because it forms part of our ancient survival mechanism, the 'flight or flight' response, chest breathing dominates when we are facing some threat. As a result of this association, chest breathing arouses feelings of stress, tension and anxiety.

For public speaking, therefore, chest breathing is entirely inappropriate since it will:

- Not provide you with enough breath to speak clearly and for a reasonable amount of time;
- Increase any anxiety you feel about speaking in public.

Abdominal breathing combined with some chest breathing will, by contrast, ensure you:

- Have sufficient air in your lungs to produce good volume without any risk of getting breathless at the wrong moment;
- Feel calmer and more in control of the situation.

118

Posture and Breathing

To ensure that you breathe rhythmically and abdominally, 'centre yourself' before starting to speak. Make certain that your weight is evenly distributed, taken up through the spine and pelvis while you are sitting down and through the legs and spine when standing.

When you become unbalanced, for instance by placing too much weight on one leg, your breathing is adversely affected.

Emotions also have a profound effect on how you breathe, especially if you are exerting great self-control to keep them hidden from view. Diaphragm and abdominal muscles tense, drawing the sternum and ribcage downwards. When you take a breath under these conditions, your shoulder and neck muscles must work harder in order to overcome the downward force. This produces fast, shallow breathing and can lead to a condition termed hyperventilation.

Smokers are particularly at risk from hyperventilation as they pull air into their lungs with a sucking motion using their face, throat and shoulder muscles instead of their diaphragm.

Speaking Anxiety and Breathing

One of the first things which happens when we become anxious is that our rate and type of breathing change. The number of breaths taken increases from the normal rate of between 12 and 16 per minute and becomes shallower so that only the upper portions of the lungs are used.

How Changes in Breathing Affect Your Emotions

The range and variety of distressing effects produced by changes in breathing are seldom fully appreciated. They include: racing heart, chest pains, dizziness and faintness (especially in young people), anxiety, panic, an inability to concentrate, diminished mental and physical performance, disturbed sleep, nightmares, increased sweating beneath the arms and on palms (emotional sweating), a feeling of unreality, visual disturbance and even hallucinations.

All these damaging effects are due to faulty breathing creating an imbalance in the ratio of carbon dioxide and oxygen in our blood.

As is well known, when inhaling we take oxygen in from the outside air and expel carbon dioxide, the waste product of metabolism, with each exhaled breath. These gases travel around the body in our bloodstream in a very tightly controlled balance. By reducing levels of carbon dioxide in the arterial blood, rapid, shallow breathing produces a condition known as hypocarbia. This occurs because, being very small, carbon dioxide molecules are able to pass in and out of nerve cells (neurones) even faster than water.

At the same time, veins constrict, reducing oxygen supplies to the brain and causing dizziness, faintness and a sense of unreality.

Holding one's breath in response to anxiety leads to a rapid build-up of carbon dioxide and produces equally distressing mental and physical consequences.

If you have experienced any of these sensations when trying to get your message across, the chances are faulty breathing is largely to blame. I shall be describing some practical methods for controlling speaker stress in Chapter Eight. For the moment, let me just emphasise the importance of sitting or standing and breathing correctly whenever you are talking to others.

This means having a relaxed but upright posture, with a straight spine and clear airway from the nose down into the lungs. Avoid sitting crunched up in your chair or, even worse, leaning forward on your elbows across the table or desk. When your weight is taken on your shoulders and elbows in this way, your shoulder muscles tense up and become involved in breathing. By forcing your abdominal organs upwards, this hunched sitting position also restricts the diaphragm and limits outward movement of the lower ribs.

When standing, distribute your weight evenly, so that you feel nicely balanced on both feet. Again make sure you are standing upright so the air can flow smoothly down into the lungs.

Breathe in and out through your nose rather than your mouth. This is because the nose is your air-conditioning plant, providing the lungs with what they most like—air which has been warmed and moistened. The nose and nasal passages also contain hairs and a sticky mucus which helps to trap dirt, dust and bacteria, so helping protect you from infections.

Breathe in by drawing down your diaphragm and allowing your stomach to push outwards while your ribcage also expands. To exhale, push your tummy muscles inwards, gently forcing the air out of your lungs.

Where poor posture has become a habit, and efficient lung and ribcage expansion are chronically restricted, you will find it helpful to carry out the following exercise. As well as training you how to breathe more effectively it will make you feel more relaxed.

Breathing Away Stress

Either lying on your back or sitting comfortably upright, close your eyes and place one hand on your chest and the other on your abdomen. Become aware of the rate and rhythm of your breathing. Notice which hand is moving, the upper or the lower one.

Inhale and exhale smoothly, slowly and deeply through

121

your nostrils. As you breathe in, picture yourself flattening the dome of your diaphragm by pushing out your lower ribs. You will feel a slight increase of pressure in the abdomen against your lower back and the floor of the pelvis. Imagine the air being drawn deeper and deeper into your lungs.

Keep your face completely relaxed while carrying out this exercise. Consciously pull in your abdominal muscles as you exhale, using your hand if necessary to push down the stomach. As you inhale become aware of your abdominal wall pushing outward.

If you have any difficulty doing this, place both hands, fingertips touching, on your stomach. When the diaphragm flattens notice how the fingertips separate as your stomach, sides and back expand.

Practise daily until this becomes your normal pattern of breathing, whether sitting, standing or lying down. Abdominal breathing infuses your blood with extra oxygen and causes the release of mood-enhancing endorphins which increase your confidence and energy levels.

SIX WAYS TO SAFEGUARD YOUR VOICE

1 Breathe correctly so you can project your voice without risk of strain.
2 Pace yourself to allow for rests.
3 Slow down your rate of speech. Not only will this spare your throat, it also makes your voice sound deeper and more authoritative.
4 Drink plenty of fluid. An ideal drink is warm water with honey or tea without milk. Never drink cold or, worse still, iced liquid.
5 Avoid milky tea or coffee before or during your presentation as the milk gums up your saliva and may cause

your voice to crack. Do not eat ice cream, cheese or other dairy products for the same reason. Toothpaste also causes problems, so do not brush your teeth immediately before a presentation.

My own favourite drink when conducting day-long workshops is hot water into which I dissolve a teaspoon of honey and a squeeze of lemon. Not only does this keep the throat nicely lubricated, it provides a little extra sugar for energy.

6 Keep your throat warm with a scarf on chilly days when outdoors to keep the larynx relaxed. Cold weather makes your vocal cords contract and become less flexible.

CHAPTER 8

Controlling Speaker Nerves

When making a presentation, your goal is not to remove all the butterflies from your stomach but to convince the butterflies to fly in formation.

Vincent Di Salvo

For many people the greatest barrier to getting their message across is fear. This can range from a mild but nonetheless uncomfortable anxiety to a blind panic. This terror may be so intense it transforms normally assertive and self-confident men and women into quivering wrecks who struggle to communicate while their minds and bodies are spiralling out of control.

As an English judge, Sir George Jessel, perceptively remarked: 'The human brain starts working the moment you are born and never stops until you stand up to speak in public.'

If the mere idea of speaking in public dries your mouth

and makes your stomach do flip-flops, take some slight comfort from the fact that you are not alone.

Everybody feels nervous to some extent when speaking in public. Even Lady Thatcher confessed to high levels of anxiety when addressing the House of Commons.

> Every time I rose to speak I would tell myself, 'Now look love, keep calm. Concentrate' . . . as I get up, yes, I'm desperately nervous. Believe you me, if I go to Wimbledon or to the Cup Final, I know exactly how those people feel when they walk out onto the pitch or onto the court—nervous, frightened to death until the game starts and then they lose themselves in the game. And that's the only way to do it.[1]

One recent survey claimed to have discovered that four out of ten Americans feared talking to an audience more than they feared dying! The trick, of course, is to avoid doing the two things simultaneously.

Those unfortunate enough to suffer a terror of opening their mouths in front of others, a condition known as *lalophobia* (from the Greek *lalia*, meaning chatter, and *phobos*, meaning fear), risk having their career prospects diminished by an inability to communicate ideas, plans and projects clearly and persuasively.

This fear of speaking in public is actually made up of several different concerns including:

● Fear of making a fool of yourself
● Fear of being in the public eye
● Fear of being judged
● Fear of feeling humiliated
● Fear of drying up

1 Margaret Thatcher, personal communication.

- Fear of not knowing your subject well enough and making silly mistakes
- Fear of being boring
- Fear of exposing oneself to a potentially hostile crowd.

Perhaps you could add to this list from your personal experience. But no matter how long it becomes, all these sources of anxiety have a common root: a fear of losing control.

Lost Control and Rising Stress

So long as we feel in command of events, challenges are regarded as stimulating rather than fear-inducing. But as the demands being made on us increase and our sense of being in control of the situation declines, stress levels start to soar.

The matrix below shows the relationship between the variables of demands, control and stress.

Where both control and demands are low (left box), so

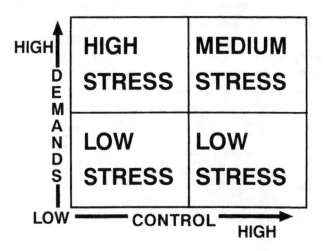

too is stress. Because we do not really care what happens, we see no reason to get worked up about the possibility of failing.

Similarly when the demands are low and we feel in control of the situation (bottom right), stress levels remain low and we cope comfortably with the challenge.

As demands increase so too does stress (top right box), but so long as we remain in control of events the level remains moderate and may actually enhance our performance.

The most stressful situation in which we can find ourselves is to face a demanding challenge without being able to maintain control over what happens.

The symptoms of public speaking nerves include some or all of the following:

- Rapidly beating heart
- Uneven breathing
- Dry mouth
- Upset stomach, nausea
- Profuse sweating
- Trembling
- Inability to think straight
- Loss of confidence and increasing self-doubt
- Negative thoughts such as 'I cannot cope with this situation.'

Imagine you have been asked to brief colleagues on a subject you know well and have spoken about many times before. Here the demands are moderate and your sense of control high, so stress remains low.

But on arriving for the meeting you find the topic has been changed. Now you will have to speak, off the cuff, on a subject with which you are far less familiar. This reduces your control over the situation and causes stress to increase.

To add to your problems a superior, who is notorious within the organisation for his acidly sarcastic criticism, has decided to attend. You know this man is never happier than when able to belittle and humiliate a subordinate. You also know he is far more expert on the subject than yourself. Your control slips further, demands increase and stress rises accordingly.

While waiting for the meeting to start, you rack your brains for the key issues and scribble some brief notes.

You can feel your heart starting to thump wildly, your mouth has gone dry and your stomach is churning. All of a sudden that hearty breakfast you gulped down an hour earlier does not seem like such a good idea—further evidence that the situation is getting even further out of control.

As you rise to speak, you become acutely aware of every eye in the room fixed on you. Glancing at your superior you see him lounging in his seat, gazing with what you interpret as malicious glee. The image of a cat licking its lips while crouching outside a mousehole flashes into your mind. Your heart beats even more wildly and you feel your legs shaking under you.

After a stumbling start things go rapidly downhill. You lose your place in the notes, repeat yourself constantly like a cracked record and ramble off the point. You sense your audience is getting confused and losing interest.

The smile in your superior's face deepens further and you know, you just know, he has spotted a blunder that will expose your lack of knowledge before the entire group. At this point your control hits zero while stress levels hit their peak.

You sit down hastily and, like a condemned man placing his head on the chopping block, wait for your reputation to be blown apart.

The Panic Spiral

What typically happens, in the panic spiral described above, is that an initial concern is allowed to get out of hand.

You may experience a slight 'kick' in the pit of your stomach as adrenaline and noradrenaline (two of the 'fight or flight' hormones) are released from glands just above the kidneys in response to a situation your brain identifies as a threat. You notice this hormone spurt and think to yourself: 'I am not sure I can cope with the situation.'

This anxious thought increases the body's fight/flight response and heightens physical arousal, making, among other things, your heart beat faster, your rate of sweating increase and your breathing become more rapid and less regular. If you really were in a life or death situation where survival depended on being able to fight or flee, these changes would greatly improve your chances. Under any other circumstances, of course, they merely signal a loss of control.

The physical symptoms trigger more gloomy thoughts about your prospects of being able to handle the situation, which serve to send your body into overdrive. As illustrated overleaf, the final outcome, unless you are able to calm down, will be panic.

Careful preparation, scripting and rehearsal will significantly improve your control over public speaking and make it easier to get your message across effectively. So too will experience of speaking to a wide variety of audiences. If you can find the time, try to get in as much public speaking practice as possible, preferably to audiences away from work.

Many organisations, such as Rotary Clubs and women's organisations, schools and colleges, residential homes and specialist interest groups, welcome outside speakers. If you

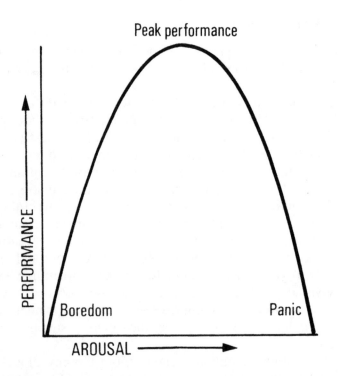

have any knowledge or skills which would make for an interesting talk, then contact as many of these outside bodies as possible and offer your services. They'll get an interesting talk at no cost to themselves, while you'll be given a variety of different audiences on which to hone your public-speaking skills.

The more experienced you are the more confident you will feel about controlling the situation and getting your message across.

George Bernard Shaw put it succinctly: 'I became a good speaker as other men became good skaters: by making a fool of myself until I got used to it.'

In addition to preparation and practice, there are a

number of practical, easily mastered techniques for bringing mental and physical stress under control; for learning,
as Vincent Di Salvo so poetically expressed it, how to
teach the butterflies to fly in formation.

A Quick Way to Unwind before You Start to Speak

Here's a 60-second procedure for reducing physical and
mental tension prior to public speaking. It can be per-
formed at your desk, in the car, or somewhere private at
the client's premises, such as the lavatory.

- Sit down as comfortably as you can and loosen any
  tight clothing, shoes, tie, belt, etc.
- Now tighten your muscles by clenching the fists,
  attempting to touch the back of your wrists to your
  shoulders, frowning and pressing the tip of your tongue
  against the roof of your mouth. At the same time stretch
  your legs, point your toes, flatten your stomach and
  inhale deeply.
- Hold this tension for a slow count to five. Feel it building up in your muscles.
- Now breathe out slowly and allow your whole body
  to go limp. Imagine you are a puppet whose strings
  have been cut. Let your shoulders drop right down and
  unclench your fingers as you flop back into the chair.
  Unfurrow your brow and let your jaw hang loose, teeth
  unclenched.
- Now take a second deep breath and hold for a slow
  count to five.
- Breathe slowly and deeply for a further 15 seconds.
  Each time you breathe out repeat the word calm, calm,
  silently and feel the relaxation flowing through your
  whole body.
- Finally soothe your nerves by imagining yourself lying

131

on the golden sand of a sun-warmed beach by a clear blue ocean. Create as vivid an image as possible and hold it for around 30 seconds.

Rehearsing in Your Imagination

In addition to rehearsing your presentation in real life, it may also be helpful to practise in the imagination.

Start by relaxing mentally and physically using the procedure described above.

After spending a few moments picturing yourself lying on a warm, sunny beach (or any other suitably soothing location) switch your mind to the situation in which you will be getting your message across.

Picture this scene as vividly as you can. See yourself communicating with your intended audience calmly and confidently. Imagine yourself making all the key points clearly and persuasively, dealing with any objections and answering questions in an authoritative and effective manner.

Try to create these scenes as clearly as possible, hearing as well as visualising what happens. Do not worry, however, if you find this rather difficult at first.

About 10 per cent of people have difficulty forming visual images and you may find that you do not need to have pictures in the mind provided your thoughts are clear.

Think about your goal in the present tense, as if it had already been achieved. Practise before going to sleep and first thing each morning. Make positive and encouraging statements about yourself.

A Quick Confidence Booster

Immediately before entering the room in which you are going to give your talk or deliver your speech do the following:

- Take five deep, slow breaths. Each time you exhale feel your mind and body becoming calmer but more alert. Imagine any anxiety flowing away from your body with the expelled air.
- Bring to mind a recent occasion when you were highly effective in getting your message across. Savour once more the sights and sounds of that success. Feel yourself being filled with energy and enthusiasm.
- Now go in and dazzle them!

Thinking on Your Feet

Few things are more likely to throw you into a spin and make you worry that you're losing control over events than the unexpected question or objection.

Imagine the following scene. You have made a lengthy speech at a company meeting and, from the warm reception your ideas were given, feel confident you have succeeded in getting your message across.

Then, just as you are giving yourself a pat on the back, Jones from accounts, your arch corporate rival, voices an objection which appears to reveal a fatal flaw in your arguments. You certainly think so and, judging by their expressions, so do many of those present. Jones, meanwhile, sits back in his seat with a triumphant smile on his face which says, 'Get out of that one!'

This is the kind of 'worst nightmare' scenario which makes the most confident speaker start panicking. The demands of the situation have suddenly shot up, while your ability to stay in control seems to have taken a sharp knock.

- Run screaming from the room?
- Throw in the towel and admit your ideas are a total waste of time?
- Jump out of the nearest window?

133

- Throw Jones out of the nearest window?
- Think on your feet?

Clearly the right answer, however tempting any of the others may seem in the panic of the moment, is the last one.

You have no choice but to talk your way out of trouble. Let me emphasise this is the correct approach even if it turns out that the dreadful Jones is absolutely correct and your ideas do, indeed, have a downside you failed to foresee.

Faced with such a challenge the first rule is DO NOT PANIC. Instead, keep the initiative by responding as follows:

Step 1: Start by thanking the person raising the objection for bringing up that particular point. This courteous response may help disarm a hostile critic and will win the audience over to you.

If the objection or question was obviously hostile and intended to make you look bad, move to step 2. If it was well intended, proceed to step 3.

Step 2: Ask the questioner or objector to repeat what he or she said. This serves two purposes: first it buys you some thinking time and second, it forces the other person to adopt a slightly different stance.

Unless he has written his question or objection down, which is unlikely, it will be virtually impossible for him to repeat his original comment word for word. Usually if he was critical and hostile on the first occasion, he will calm down somewhat when asked to repeat the remark.

Step 3: Pause and organise. This is another time-buying phase. Never be tempted to respond instantly, even if you immediately know what to say. Pausing makes your answer appear more thoughtful, considered and worthy of serious consideration.

Learn to stay silent while thinking. Avoid voiced pauses such as 'ah', 'um', 'er', since these merely make you sound uncertain and lacking in confidence.

Step 4: Repeat the objection or question, saying something along these lines: 'If I have understood you correctly, the point you are making is that . . .'

Always use a neutral expression such as 'the point' or 'the matter', never words like 'objection', 'problem', 'disadvantage', 'difficulty' or anything else which suggests there are negative aspects to your proposals and would only impress onto the minds of your listeners the fact that you too regard it in this light.

Using reflective listening not only ensures you fully understand the point raised, but also helps defuse any 'ego involvement' the individual has attached to his comments.

Many people seem to enjoy criticising and condemning others for its own sake. Instead of listening to what's being said in an open, objective state of mind, they are busy looking out for reasons why those proposals should not or cannot be put into practice. Having worked hard at being negative, they have a strong, emotional attachment to their viewpoint.

If you simply shoot the objection down in flames, they are likely to become increasingly hostile and more and more firmly entrenched behind a barricade of prejudices.

By rephrasing the objection or question in your own words, you stop it from being 'their' property and place it in the public arena. Under these circumstances they are less likely to want to defend it to the death.

Step 5: Ask for any other objections to be raised at that time by saying something along these lines: 'OK, I understand what you are saying. In addition to that point do you have any other reasons for not accepting my proposals?'

This is important since, if you do not bring all the objector's concerns out into the open at that time, you may find yourself caught up in a seemingly endless flow of objections. If he wants to raise a second or third point, return to step 1 and repeat the process.

Step 6: When all the objections have been brought out into the open and stated in your own words, clarify the situation by summarising the main items on which there is agreement and disagreement. At this point the objector will either agree with your summary or raise further objections, which means going back to the beginning again.

Once all the objections have been dealt with in this way, your next step is to persuade him to see both positions more objectively.

Start by offering workable alternatives which are less satisfactory than those originally proposed to those parts of your proposals to which objections have been made. By getting the person to compare a number of alternatives, you help him to shift from a strong emotional commitment to a more logical appraisal of his objections.

Outline all the available options. Sketch their advantages and disadvantages in a calm, rational manner. If the other person has proposals to make and they are useful, then modify them slightly before passing them back for consideration.

In this way you can ensure that he remains objective about the ideas since, because they are no longer entirely his own creation, there is less emotional attachment. Introduce facts and figures which support your own proposals and counter the objections at this point. But do so in a restrained manner. Reserve your shots for appropriate targets.

You will not experience loss of control by accepting ideas and suggestions so long as you always restate these in your own words before incorporating them into the overall plan.

When answering a question, do so by responding rather

than simply replying. This means elaborating on the question by adding additional items of information. These can be linked into your response by means of a phrase such as 'the main point at issue' or 'my primary objective'.

If members of the audience want the response elaborated this provides them with an opportunity for asking further questions. But be careful never to overwhelm the audience with information. Never end on an excuse. When you come to the end of your response simply *stop*.

Step 7: If you do not like the question then provide a better one. This is a particularly useful technique with media interviews (see Chapter Fifteen). Do this by:

- Asking a question of your own;
- Requesting clarification;
- Asking for a definition or providing your own;
- Clarifying the point yourself.

Politicians are past masters (and mistresses) of thinking on their feet. Listen to political interviews and notice how often they use the techniques described above.

Knowledge Conquers Fear

The motto of the Parachute Regiment, 'Knowledge Conquer Fear', offers excellent advice to people faced with the problem of conquering their own fears in order to communicate successfully.

By following these ten tips, you should find it a great deal easier to reduce your stress level to a point where it improves rather than impedes your presentation, makes you feel alert and full of energy, instead of fearful and ready to flee.

1 Do your homework thoroughly before communicating an important message. The better prepared, knowledgeable and experienced you are, the greater will be your

137

sense of control over the situation. And the more control you have, the less likely it is that sudden panic will prevent you from getting your message across.

2   If you start feeling tense in the run up to the presentation, find somewhere quiet and spend a few minutes relaxing.

3   Imagine yourself getting your message across successfully, or use the memory of a previously effective presentation to boost confidence.

4   If you have to talk in unfamiliar surroundings, try to scout them out a day or so before. Should that not be possible, arrive early and have a look at the room. Stand where you will be standing and test out the acoustics. Get a friend or colleague to stand at the back to make sure you can easily be heard.

Make it your turf. Because we all naturally feel more on edge in strange surroundings, familiarising yourself with the venue in this way will take the edge off your nerves.

5   Remember that audiences only get what you give them. They cannot read your mind or see the butterflies in your stomach. Provided you appear calm and in command, that is how they will perceive you. It doesn't matter that you are trembling a little on the inside provided you refrain from trembling on the outside.

6   When you speak before a group make your voice sound full of confidence and authority. It will not only impress your listeners but make you feel more relaxed and in control.

7   Never take a couple of quick drinks to calm your nerves. Alcohol is a powerful sedative which works by dulling the brain. You may think it helps, but it does not.

8   If you have a lectern, start off standing behind it and lightly holding the edges for support. I emphasise the

word 'lightly', because some nervous speakers grip the edge so tightly you can see the blood draining from their knuckles. The lectern will provide you with additional support—and 'cover'—during the first few minutes as you get into your stride.

Most speakers find their nerves leave them and their confidence builds once they have got under way. When you feel sufficiently confident, try stepping away from the lectern (you can still hold on with one hand if it helps) so that your listeners can see more of you. Opening up your body in this way greatly improves your ability to communicate in the relaxed and conversational way which audiences prefer.

9   If panicky feelings arise during the course of your speech do not be tempted to rush through to the end. Speaking faster will only upset your breathing and increase your anxiety. Pause for a few seconds while you regain your composure and then continue.

10 If you are going to invite questions at the end of your talk, but are concerned people may be reluctant to speak up, plant one or two questions in the audience among friends or colleagues. Not only will having a couple of questions to which you know the answers— after all you wrote them—increase your confidence, it will also stimulate other members of your audience to ask questions of their own, so avoiding that embarrassing silence which so often follows a request for questions.

CHAPTER 9

Getting On and Getting Off

Great is the art of the beginning, but greater is the art of ending.

Henry Wadsworth Longfellow

Students on a crime-writing course were told of the importance of a dramatic opening which captured their readers' attention and compelled them to read on. 'The most popular topics are religion, royalty, sex and crime,' the tutor explained. 'Try to work at least one of them into your first page.'

One student responded with: '"My God",' gasped the princess, "I'm pregnant. Who done it?"'

Without resorting to these extremes, you should strive to make your first words grab your listeners' attention in order to make them want to listen on.

For most speakers, knowing how to get going and how to finish are the two trickiest parts of getting their message across.

One approach to getting going is to follow the speakers' adage I quoted earlier of 'telling 'em what you are going to tell 'em, telling 'em and telling 'em what you told them'. As well as previewing the main parts of your message, the opening should contain some attention-grabbing device which ensures your audience will listen to what follows.

Various types of ear-catching opening are described below. Memorise one or two of these standard openings and closings, for example the 'good news/bad news' routine and the 'summary' tactic. These will provide you with off-the-peg 'starts' and 'stops' which will make even impromptu speeches (see Chapter Ten) sound polished and professional.

Getting your message across can be likened to a Shuttle space mission. What people best remember from such flights are the launch, the moment when a crucial part of the mission is completed and the safe touchdown.

The Shuttle launch corresponds to your opening comments, remarks designed to arouse interest and evoke sympathy from your listeners. The strong central message you have to get across is your mission, while touchdown is an ending which leaves your audience motivated and persuaded.

Knowing how you are going to begin and end a message significantly increases your confidence as you rise to speak. It also ensures you get cleanly and quickly into the body of your message in the shortest amount of time.

By communicating in this brisk and efficient manner you will impress your listeners with your knowledge, authority and confidence, so making it more likely they pay attention and feel persuaded by what you say.

GETTING STARTED

While it is always better to get straight to your main message than to embark on an aimless preamble which makes you sound pompous or boring or both, in most cases an ice-breaking opening is advised.

This sets the mood for what is to follow and gives your listeners time to focus on you as a new speaker and tune in to what you will be saying. It accustoms them to your tone and accent (especially important if you have a strong regional one), appearance, expression, posture and gesture.

It gives *you* a chance to assess them, to get a feeling for their mood, and to tune in to the kind of message to which they will prove most responsive.

The 'ice-breaker' also helps you to calm down before getting into the main part of your message, to overcome any last-minute nerves and to loosen up your larynx. The most experienced of speakers can find their voices tightening up somewhat when they first start speaking.

Finally, the opening will allow you to establish the right volume so that your audience can hear you comfortably, as well as getting into the rhythm and pace of your speech.

A word of warning: never start by apologising for any lack of preparedness or confidence in your ability to deliver a persuasive message. Some speakers do this in an attempt to win over their audiences' sympathy and understanding for the confused ramblings which are to follow. Even when the tactic succeeds in winning you the 'pity' vote, it can only diminish their trust and belief in your message.

While every opening will be different, varying according to the type of message being delivered, the type of audience on the receiving end and the nature of the occasion, three cardinal rules should always be strictly adhered to:

1   Never drone on.

2   Inform by talking *to* rather than *at* your listeners.
3   Entertain, in a manner appropriate to the occasion.

Six Classic Openings

1 *Use a Startling Fact*

When I started working as a journalist, an editor gave me this thumbnail definition of what makes a good news story. 'There are,' he told me, 'two types of facts. Those I didn't know but which do *not* surprise me when I'm told, and those I didn't know which astonish me when I'm told!'

It is the second type which will provide an attention-grabbing opening for your messages—both spoken and written.

The fact or facts you choose may be taken from your own professional background, from the organisation which you are addressing or from the press. Here are a couple from speeches I have delivered to multinational companies recently.

From a presentation on 'Managing Change':

The Fortune 500, a list of the 500 largest corporations in the USA, was first compiled in 1955. Forty years on, if we look at the top 25 on that original list, we find that five have gone out of business, six are no longer even in the top 25, and two are not even in the top 100.

Yet, in their day, these were the biggest, brightest and best companies in the world. They had a total command of their market positions. So how on earth could they ever have failed?

On another occasion, while making a keynote presentation to a company on the impact of technology on employee psychology, I learned it was the chairman's birthday. I asked my assistant to buy a birthday card with a microchip inside which played 'Happy Birthday' when the card was opened.

After being introduced, I wished the CEO a happy anniversary and then played the card. Setting it down, I explained:

> That card contains more computing power than existed in the whole world prior to 1950. The home video camera on which your chairman's spouse recorded her birthday party contains more processing power than the IBM 360 machine which gave birth to the computer age. And the Sega Saturn gamemaker, which she gave to her teenage son for his birthday, has a processor more powerful than the 1976 Cray Supercomputer, a machine so costly and complicated it could only be used by the scientific élite. Those are some of the measures by which we can judge how far computer technology has advanced over the past few decades.

Notice that here I combined a demonstration with my opening words. Showing people something, at any stage in your presentation, can powerfully reinforce your message.

2 A Strong and Relevant Anecdote

Providing it is directly relevant to your message, a striking and memorable story can provide an excellent opening which sets the scene for the main message in your presentation. Here's one from an introduction by E. S. Woolard, Jr, formerly chairman of E. I. du Pont de Nemours and Company, given at a *Business Week* symposium of chief executive officers:

144

Last month in China, I had lunch with the chairman of a firm in the Guandong Province. The firm's leadership comes from old economic planning groups in the Communist Party. When given the freedom to move to Hong Kong and develop trade and business for their province, they built a $1.5 billion business in 14 years from scratch. They claim it is very profitable, and the shares they issued increased ten times in the past few years. I asked the executive to describe his company's areas of business.

He responded, 'Anywhere we can make money.' I came back from that trip convinced that China will grow and profits will be made.

3 A Striking Example

This can be serious or humorous, factual or in the form of metaphor or simile.

Opening his speech on energy trends to a Clean Coal Technology Conference, held in Chicago in 1994, Thomas A. Altmeyer of the National Coal Association gave numerous examples illustrating an increasing demand for coal and electric power in the US economy:

- Demand for electric power grew by 88 per cent.
- Power generation with coal grew by 133 per cent.
- The coal-burn for power generation grew by 154 per cent.
- The coal share of power generation rose from 46 per cent to 57 per cent.

After citing further examples, he concluded his introduction by saying: 'The coal-burn for electric power set new records in 20 of the last 23 years, and this year will make it 21 of 24.'[1]

1 Quoted in the *Journal of Executive Speeches*, the bimonthly journal of *The Executive Speaker Newsletter*, vol. 9, no. 6, June 1995.

4 Paying a Compliment

We all enjoy being praised. It's only human nature. Being human, your listeners will respond positively to positive comments about themselves, their achievements, their organisation, their city or their country.

Here's a fine example of this type of opening from James R. Paul, president and chief executive officer of the Coastal Corporation.

> It's a pleasure to be here. The first thing I want to do is compliment you on being creative enough to still be around after the last several years. Believe me, to stay alive in this energy business you have to be nimble.[1]

5 A Challenging Question

A surprising rhetorical question involves your listeners from the start by getting them to think about your topic even before you get to the main points. If the answer is amusing, you'll also help relax your audience by showing you intend to entertain as well as inform.

Speaking on quality to the Virginia Foundation for Independent Colleges, R. Alan Brogan, vice-president of quality management for Norfolk Southern Corporation, uses a series of questions to challenge his audience:

> Let me ask how many of you are confident that your institutions now provide the best education that you can possibly afford?

1 James R. Paul, 'Remarks on the Economy and the Oil and Gas Industry: The Price We Pay', delivered at Oil and Gas Conference, Houston, 16 December, 1992.

146

According to Richard Rosett, dean of the College of Business at Rochester Institute of Technology and an avid proponent of total quality management in higher education, one quarter of the classes taught by any college or university are ineffective, unnecessary, unfocused, or simply undesirable.

Could that possibly hold true with your institution?

How long do you think Norfolk Southern could survive if 25 per cent of the freight we delivered was lost or damaged?[1]

6 The Classic Humorous Opening

This is one of the oldest and most traditional ways of breaking the ice.

When done well it is a highly effective way of starting all but the most serious of messages. Your audience feels relaxed and entertained and looks forward to the rest of your message.

When done badly, however, it can let you down with a bump, creating embarrassment rather than amusement and, if the joke is ill-chosen, hostility or distaste from your listeners.

I shall be discussing humour in more detail in Chapter Ten. But here let me emphasise that any stories you tell, or quotations you use, must be:

- Relevant to your message. I remember, at one of my workshops on speaking skills, a senior manager began a talk on sales techniques by saying:

1 R. Alan Brogan, 'Remarks on Quality', delivered at Ilot Springs, Virginia, 2 August, 1992. Quoted in *The Executive Speaker Newsletter*, vol. 14, no. 10, October 1993.

'A man walking to an airport departure lounge turned to his wife and said: 'I wish I had our grand piano with me.' 'Why?' his wife asked, bewildered. 'Because I left our passports and tickets on it.'

He then moved directly to the main part of his off-the-cuff presentation, without further reference to the story, which, it quickly transpired, had nothing to do with anything that was to follow. He'd merely responded to my advice on starting with a joke by telling the only 'joke' he knew.

● Appropriate to the occasion. I shall deal in a moment with types of humour to avoid.

Mark Twain's definition of a banker as 'a fellow who lends you his umbrella when the sun is shining and wants it back the minute it starts to rain' is a good joke to tell in some situations, but a convention of bankers is probably not one of them!

● Fresh. If you heard it last night on TV then the chances are a large proportion of your audience will have as well. Also beware of using a joke which has been doing the rounds of your organisation. If the audience hasn't already heard it, the chances are one of the speakers before you will have used it.

Used properly, any of these six openings will help launch your message, rewarding you with not only attention but also appreciation. In addition, you can sometimes use:

References to the Setting or Situation

The last time I addressed a crowd this large I sensed during my speech that something was wrong. So I asked if everyone could hear all right. A gentleman at the back stood up and said he hadn't been able to hear a thing. Right away, four people in the front got up and moved to the back?[1]

Good News/Bad News

I began one of my own presentations on the need for vision in shaping corporate destiny during times of change by describing an airline flying through a blizzard among the Alpine peaks when the pilot tells his passengers: 'I have good news and bad news. The bad news is we are flying too low through the mountains and I haven't the slightest idea where we are headed. The good news is we are going there at 600 mph.'

I went on to draw an analogy between the lost pilot, his startled passengers and the approach to change taken by many managers.

ENDING ON A HIGH

Six Classic Closes

Just tailing off and sitting down at the end of an otherwise interesting and persuasive speech creates a sense of anti-climax which can spoil all that has gone before.

Getting out of your message effectively is as essential to getting your message across successfully as starting well.

1 UPS chairman and chief executive officer, Kent C. Nelson, in remarks entitled 'The Three R's of the Business Education', delivered before the South Carolina Governor's Conference on Education.

1 The Surprise Ending

Startle your audience by an unexpected conclusion or comment.

> At this point, I will not say 'in conclusion' because there is none. The fun is just starting. I'll be interested to hear your ideas. I'll just close with Voltaire's remark that 'the great consolation in life is to say what one thinks'. If nothing else, I've experienced that consolation today.[1]

2 The Summary

This is a traditional and satisfactory if not very exciting way of ending your message. Its value is in aiding recall through the 'recency effect' discussed above. When you have insufficient time to prepare, it is probably the easiest, and certainly the safest way to conclude.

3 The Joke

The old show business adage to 'leave them laughing' applies to many types of message as well. But make sure any story or quote you do use satisfies the criteria described above.

4 An Upbeat or Uplifting Exhortation

On some occasions, you need to leave your audience inspired as much as informed. Here your choice of words and language needs to be elevating and arousing. Conclud-

---

1 Alan M. Perlman, PhD, 'The Power and the Gory: Words DO Mean Something! Don't They?', delivered before the Chicago Speechwriters Forum, Illinois, 6 June, 1995. Quoted in *The Executive Speaker Newsletter*, vol. 17, no. 1, January 1996.

ing a speech entitled 'Law in Times of Turbulence' given before the Catholic University Law School in Washington, DC, Mary Ann Glendon, a professor of law at Harvard University, said:

> May you be at all times, even at personal sacrifice, a champion of fairness and due process, in court or out, and for all, whether the powerful and envied, or the helpless, or the hated, or the oppressed. Good luck and Godspeed![1]

5   A Call to Action

This is a command to 'walk and talk', to turn words heard at a meeting, conference or similar gathering into positive action which will improve your organisation's per-formance.

A close which I often employ under such circumstances uses a photograph of me jumping out of an aircraft at 6,000 feet. I explain my hobby is sky-diving and that, in parachuting, we have a saying: 'It won't mean a thing if you don't pull the string.' I then conclude by pointing out that the same applies in their organisation, where action rather than words alone will win the day.

6   A Final Compliment

Leave members of your audience feeling good about them-selves and they are more likely to remember what you told them. Here's an excellent example of a complimentary ending built around a final joke:

> Let me close by telling you about the kamikaze pilot who flew 23 missions.

1 Quoted in *The Executive Speaker Newsletter*, vol. 15, no. 7, July 1994.

'How can that be?' asked the reporter who interviewed him. 'You're supposed to crash the airplane
into the enemy ship. How could you fly 23 missions?'

'Well,' said the pilot, 'I had the motivation. I just
didn't have the commitment.'

What I see here tonight is talent, motivation and
commitment . . . which add up to success. I congratu-
late you all on your achievements . . . I know there
will be many more to come . . . and, in whatever
career you choose, I wish you the very best.[1]

Knowing when to stop talking is as vital to your success
in getting a message across as knowing how to start and
what to say. By going on too long you can snatch defeat
from the jaws of victory. Always leave your audience
wanting more rather than longing for less. As a Yiddish
proverb puts it: 'If you keep on talking, you will end up
saying what you didn't intend to say.'

1 E. R. Guardia, 'Why Not a Career in Food?' delivered at 4-H Awards
Dinner, Chicago, 7 December, 1992.

CHAPTER 10

To Script or Not to Script? That is the Question

Three things matter in a speech: who says it, how he says it, and what he says and, of the three, the last matters the least.
    John Morley, English editor, biographer, and statesman

It's nightmare time. While you were still sitting down, the message you wanted to get across was crystal clear in your mind. You knew exactly how to start, how to develop your key points and how to conclude with a rousing flow of oratory which would render your listeners spellbound.

Once on your feet and gazing around at the expectant faces, you suddenly find yourself speechless instead of spellbinding.

Every thought, idea, proposal and plan has vanished from your mind. Of your carefully crafted message not a trace remains and you can feel the surges of panic threatening to overwhelm you. For a few moments you stand there as if in a trance, mouth opening and closing silently like a beached fish. Finally a few garbled sounds emerge from your lips, but instead of golden words you manage to produce only gurgles.

I exaggerate of course. It's rarely if ever as bad as that, although it can certainly seem that horrendous to any speaker unfortunate enough to be struck down by what stage people call a 'dry'.

Drying up in front of an audience is something every professional performer dreads, and most experience it at least once in their career.

In the days before prompters, Shakespearian actors and actresses devised two ways of getting themselves out of trouble if they suffered a memory blank on stage. The first was to learn a piece of spoof Shakespeare. Although the lines they painstakingly memorised had never come within a hundred miles of the Bard's quill pen, they sounded as if they had. What's more, they were written so that you could fit them into any of his dramas without many in the audience being any the wiser.

As soon as the actual words deserted them, the actors slipped effortlessly into the spoof quotation and continued on 'autopilot' while racking their brains for the right words. Although confusing to fellow players, who had no idea where to pick up the cue, this was generally considered an acceptable strategy for overcoming a temporary dry.

Much less acceptable, however, was the alternative tactic, practised by some famous actors and actresses when they dried, of stating in a loud and meaningful manner, 'But more of this anon', before striding off to the wings where they would hastily consult the text, while their stranded fellow thespians struggled on as best they could.

Away from the professional stage, speakers dry for two

main reasons. The first is that they have tried to memorise a lengthy script and discovered, too late, they cannot do it.

Unless you have an exceptionally well-trained memory, such as is found among show-business professionals who spend their lives learning lines, it is extremely difficult and highly risky to attempt to memorise a speech and deliver it word perfect before an audience.

The second cause of drying arises from a belief held by many inexperienced speakers that they can ad lib with little or no preparation or rehearsal.

In my experience, the more senior an executive the more likely it is that he or she will refuse to prepare or rehearse. Many seem to suffer from the delusion that the right words will flow from their lips when the moment arises. Sadly it seldom works out that way. Instead the audience is usually compelled to suffer a series of rambling, disjointed and disconnected ideas, often laced by a series of poorly told and frequently inappropriate jokes.

Of course many corporate speakers are also excellent at delivering a powerful message off the cuff. They have the ability, honed over years of practice, to deliver impromptu speeches in a lively, amusing and logical manner. The fact that they have not anguished over every word gives their messages a relaxed and conversational air which is the essence of effective and persuasive communications. But this level of mastery, like any polished skill, does not come easily. To perfect it demands natural talent combined with extensive practice.

Meanwhile, for the rest of us, there are a number of practical things that can be done to achieve the *appearance* of presenting in an informal and conversational manner without the risks inherent in just standing up and hoping for the best.

I call this method the Swan System of impromptu speaking, not after the Bard of Avon, but because like the swan, the serene and effortless manner in which you get your message across belies the hard work going on just below the surface.

Let's start by looking at the impromptu communication, that is a message you were not aware of having to get across until a short time before actually doing so.

THE SWAN SYSTEM OF IMPROMPTU SPEAKING

Step 1: Do not panic. However short the notice, rise to the challenge in a calm and purposeful manner. See it as an opportunity to excel rather than a chance to get egg all over your face.

Step 2: This depends on how long you actually have to prepare.

Even with an impromptu speech there are usually warnings that you may be called upon to say a few words. If you have to do so regularly with little prior warning, prepare in advance.

Write brief prompts on index cards (see cue cards below) which cover the main topics on which you are likely to have to deliver a talk. These cards should not contain a complete script—not even in summary form—but merely sufficient prompts to get you started and to get you finished.

If you are utterly unprepared by the request to speak, and have only a matter of minutes to scribble a few words, construct an *ideogram*. This is a device which encourages the flow of ideas around a topic far more effectively than jotting down notes in the usual manner.

Take a sheet of plain, unlined paper (the back of a menu will do if you are called upon to speak off the cuff after a meal) and note down two or three words (no more) which describe the main point on which you are to speak. Write this in the middle of the paper and draw an oval around it.

Now think about anything your main point brings to mind. Write these fresh thoughts around the first heading. Circle each and link it with a line to the original oval.

Taking the new points in turn, consider what ideas each of these trigger. As before, note these points down, ring

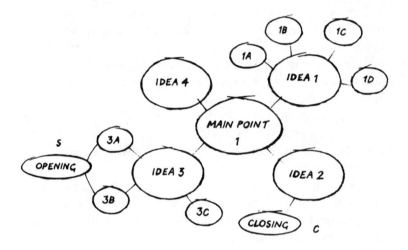

them and draw lines connecting them to the 'seed' thought.

From the ideogram identify the four building blocks of your speech:

1   The main point
2   Supporting material
3   Opening
4   Closing.

Number as '1' the oval containing your first point. Next find the supporting ideas linked logically to the main point and number those ovals accordingly. Find a starting point and somewhere to end. Identify these ovals with 'S' for start and 'C' for close.

In a very short space of time you will have created a blueprint from which to build your speech. It will show you where to begin, how to develop a logical and meaningful argument in support of your key point, and where to end. The ideogram will also ensure nothing vital is missed out and nothing inessential is included.

This same approach works even when you are given literally no time to prepare, when you have to work out what you are going to say while rising to your feet or walking over to the lectern. Focus on identifying the main point and never be tempted to speak until you have this clearly in mind.

Step 3: On rising to your feet pause for a moment (this advice applies to all types of presentation) both to collect your thoughts and to allow everybody to focus their attention on you.

Take a deep breath before starting to speak, and deliver your first words clearly and calmly. Provided you know your subject, you will find the ideas flow easily once that starting hurdle has been surmounted.

Step 4: If you dry up, do not panic. Just pause. Remember you can hold a pause for at least four seconds without your audience being aware that anything is going wrong.

Do not be tempted to fill silences with 'umms' or any other meaningless sounds. Just stay silent and glance around the room. While doing so think about anything your last remark reminds you of.

Fall back on any anecdotes or examples which come to mind—with luck you will be able to dredge up one relevant to your message, but in an emergency almost anything will do. While telling this well-rehearsed story, relax and allow your mind to dwell calmly on the subject under discussion. You will soon find that, with the pressure removed, those mislaid words and ideas come flooding back, allowing you to pick up the speech where you left off.

When you have time to prepare your message more carefully, a number of options may be available to remind you of what you want to say. The question now becomes: 'To Script or Not to Script?' So let's look at some of the advantages and disadvantages of the different methods available.

Reading from a Script

Advantages: No ideas or key points are missed. Since you wrote the speech you know exactly what you're going to say and how. If you are nervous it may boost your confidence to follow the printed page.
Disadvantages: Unless you are *very* experienced, reading a script will sound—and look—stilted. Reading from the page makes it far harder, especially for inexperienced speakers, to give the audience sufficient eye contact.

How to Do it

Have the script typed in a large font size. Make sure each page ends on a complete sentence. You do not want to have to turn a page to find out how to finish a sentence. Use white paper and black type which give you maximum legibility under what may be low light levels behind the lectern.

Rehearse until you know your lines virtually by heart. This means you can glance down, take in a whole sentence or paragraph at a time, then give members of your audience eye contact as you speak those words.

Do not staple or clip the pages together, since this makes it harder to turn the pages. The best method, when speaking from behind a table, desk or lectern, is simply to drop the finished page to the floor. This safeguards you from accidentally going back over a page you have already read. This becomes worrying if your audience gets restless as you repeat yourself, highly embarrassing if it utterly fails to notice you are doing so! Only do this if you are sure the audience cannot be distracted by watching the pages fall. Otherwise simply slide the completed page to one side.

Only speak from a script when you absolutely have to, for instance on occasions when the choice of words has to be extremely precise for legal or similar reasons. If you have complicated statistics or similar facts to present, script those parts but use cue cards (see below) to lend a more natural delivery for the less complex parts of your message

Speaking Off the Cuff

Advantages: When done well it sounds natural and conversational. You have the flexibility to adjust your presentation as you go along to match audience response.
Disadvantages: As discussed above, speakers tend not to prepare as well, believing ideas will flow easily. As I mentioned above, this leaves them in danger of groping for words, stumbling and confusing the audience. There is also a serious risk of straying beyond the allocated time.

Using Cue Cards

Advantages: This is the method favoured by most professional and experienced speakers. Cue cards combine the comfort of a script with the conversational style of an off-the-cuff presentation.
Disadvantages: Requires practice. There is a risk of losing your way unless the cards are carefully constructed and well rehearsed.

How to Do it

Write or type key points from your script onto small cards. The 3″ x 5″ index size which can easily be carried in the pocket and held in the hand is most suitable.

If hand printing the text, use a large typeface with double or even triple spacing. Avoid abbreviations which may cause you confusion. There should be no more than four lines on each card, with a maximum of six words in each. Write in large, easy to read block capitals.

Punch a hole in one of the corners of each card and thread a loop of string through them. If you happen to drop them, you can easily pick them up in one piece and in the right order, rather than scrabbling around for a dozen cards and trying to sort them into sequence again as your audience grows increasingly restless.

An alternative to cards, used by some professional presenters, is to cue yourself via your visual aids (see Chapter Eleven). Provided you have rehearsed your presentation thoroughly, the bullet points on transparencies plus brief notes on the overhead projection mounts will be sufficient reminders.

WHEN, WHERE AND HOW TO EMPLOY HUMOUR

There are many reasons for adding a sprinkling of humour to your talk. When you do your audience will:

- Respect you more;
- Listen with greater attention;
- Remember more of what you say.

Six Ways of Using Humour Effectively

1   Use it sparingly. Comedy must enhance your message not become an irrelevant addition to it.
2   Only tell anecdotes, jokes or quotes which you personally find funny and when you understand why they are funny. Never be tempted to tell a joke which somebody assures you is hilarious even though the punch line escapes you.
3   If you have doubts about any joke drop it. If a joke makes you feel even slightly uncomfortable, telling it will only increase your anxiety.
4   Be certain of the punch line of your story. Know the wording. Know the timing.
5   Always tell stories in your own style. Never simply memorise them from a joke book. Rework them into a format which fits your natural style of delivery.
6   Respect your audience. Approach it as if it was a gathering of old friends and your humour will flow naturally and effortlessly. Just as you would never, under those circumstances, tell a joke likely to upset or offend them, afford audiences the same courtesy.

WHEN YOU ARE PART OF A TEAM

So far I have talked about getting your message across by yourself. But there may be occasions when you do so as one of a team. Under these circumstances it is essential to rehearse together at least twice before the event.

The first rehearsal is a run-through during which all the main points of the message which must be communicated are identified and assigned to those responsible for presenting them.

Between the first and second rehearsal, you will probably think of additional points which can be discussed with other members of your team before the next run-through.

This second rehearsal is vital and time must be set aside for it no matter how much pressure you are all under. Discuss new ideas and work out where they need to be introduced. Now run through the presentation, including all visuals, preferably before an audience who can provide feedback.

Always Rehearse the Qs and As

Brief your audience to ask challenging and difficult questions. Discuss who will answer these and how best to respond to such questions. Rehearsing the questions and answers sessions in this way helps you all:

● Feel prepared, so increasing self-confidence;
● Deal with the genuine questions professionally.

CHOOSING THE RIGHT TIME OF DAY

If the message you want to get across is sufficiently important and you can exercise control over when it is to be delivered, picking the right time of day can make a big difference to its reception.

Because our energy levels and attention span vary considerably over the course of the day, a message which is indifferently received at one time may be welcomed and acted upon if communicated earlier or later.

The worst times to choose are immediately before and just after lunch, and again in the late afternoon. The best times are around one hour after starting work, once the immediate panic of the morning has subsided, and around 3 p.m. At these times most people are at their most alert and receptive to new ideas.

163

CHAPTER 11

Eyes Have It, the Power of Visual Aids

I hear and I learn, I see and I understand.
Chinese proverb

Here's a simple experiment that clearly demonstrates the dominance of our eyes over our ears.

Ask a group of people to follow the instructions below while you demonstrate them:

Raise your left hand.

Stick up your thumb.

Form an 'O' between your thumb and first finger.

Uncurl your thumb and finger then touch the top of your head with your index finger.

Touch your chin.

As you issue this last instruction, touch not your chin but your cheek. You'll find that 99 per cent of people follow your visual example rather than your spoken command.

Research suggests that we remember around 80 per cent of what we see, but only some 15 per cent of what we hear.

As the table below shows, combining words and images also creates stronger and longer-lasting recall of information.

Type of message	After 3 hours	After 3 days
Tell only	70%	10%
Show only	72%	20%
Show and tell	85%	65%

Other benefits you will gain by using visual aids to help get your message across include:

- Increasing the chances of agreement when proposing a plan of action;
- Reducing the amount of time needed to get your message across by as much as 40 per cent;
- Communicating complex messages not only faster but more accurately;
- Arousing and holding your audience's interest;
- Adding variety and interest to an otherwise serious message;
- Cutting across language barriers. This is clearly of great help when talking to an international or multicultural audience whose first language is not your own.

While I believe visual aids enhance almost every type

of message, except the most informal and light-hearted 'after dinner' type of speeches, there are occasions when it is essential to use visual aids:

- When making statistical comparisons. It is very hard for people to hold two sets of facts or figures in their minds while comparing them. Being able to read the information makes the task easier and the interpretation far more reliable.
- When introducing data arranged in chronological order, such as year-on-year productivity increases, where one has to remember information from one segment to the next.
- When imparting information previously known only to you. People given unfamiliar information find it very helpful to be able to refer back and check their understanding of what has just been said.
- When delivering a controversial message which many may doubt without supporting evidence in the form of visual information. As they say, 'seeing is believing'.
- When your message includes quotes, lists, statistical information, trends. All these data are very hard to remember without visual reinforcement.

CREATING HIGH-IMPACT VISUALS

When you are preparing any type of visual aid keep the following points in mind:

- Focus on only *one* idea per visual.
- Choose the text carefully; the fewer words the better.
- Avoid creating cluttered visuals. Concise bullet points are easier to understand than long sentences. Avoid clip-art embellishments unless they significantly enhance the interest of your message and so contribute to the attention it receives.

- Underline the title and separate each key idea presented.
- Make certain that every visual contains a clear message. Never be tempted to use charts or tables unless they are central to the points being made.
- Never begin or end your presentation with a visual. The audience needs to see you and form an impression of you as a speaker rather than simply look at the visuals.
- Always start, and end, with the room lights up so that you can communicate non-verbally (see Chapter Twelve) as well as verbally with your listeners. This is particularly important when using 35 mm slides which require a darkened room.

I remember attending a talk given by a famous Arctic explorer with a fascinating tale to tell. His graphic account of ordeals endured on his numerous expeditions made for compelling listening. He illustrated this tale with scores of dramatic colour slides.

Unfortunately he spoke from behind a lectern, so that his features were illuminated only by a dim lectern lamp and faint light splashing onto him from the screen. He began his talk in semi-darkness and ended in the gloom, simply striding from the platform as soon as his talk was finished.

As a result he made far less impact on his large audience than the nature and content of his talk deserved. Despite all the drama and the heroics, many of his audience were left feeling let down by the fact he had never come to life as a human being.

TYPES OF VISUAL AIDS

There are six main types of visual aid which are commonly used to get one's message across to groups large and small.

1 Hand-outs
2 Flip charts
3 Overhead projectors (OHPs)
4 Slide projectors
5 Computer-generated images.

We'll examine each of these in turn to see their advantages and disadvantages, together with the best methods of creating them.

Hand-outs

Advantages: Easy to produce and pass around. Can contain far more supporting information, facts, figures, charts and graphs than it is usually possible to communicate verbally. Save your listeners from being distracted by writing notes and allow them to give you their complete attention. It is often helpful to include copies of any slides or OHP material which you are using to illustrate your message. *Disadvantages*: Few. The main snag is that people may read the hand-out while you are speaking, and so be distracted from the message. Unless there are good reasons to the contrary, only pass around hand-outs at the end of your talk.

How to Produce Professional Hand-outs

Check the lay-out, spelling and grammar carefully. Always ask a third party to read your copy since it is very hard for the author to spot mistakes: we tend to see what we expect to see instead of what is actually there.

Keep the amount of information provided to a minimum.

People are more likely to take the time to read through two or three sheets than a thick tome. Only include facts and figures clearly relevant to your message.

Hand-outs should be typed, double spaced, on white paper.

Flip Charts

Advantages: Flexible, easy to use and readily available. Allow you to display information obtained from your audience. Not suitable when there are more than 40 in the audience.
Disadvantages: Time-consuming to write out during your presentation, which is also distracting for your audience. Flip charts are best largely prepared beforehand with only a few key words being added during your talk. Marker pens dry out rapidly if left uncapped, so always check those available to make certain they write properly before starting your talk.

How to Prepare Flip Charts

Follow the 5 x 5 rule. There should be no more than five lines per page with a maximum of five words in each line.

Use green marker pens when presenting in low light levels since they have maximum luminosity. Avoid blue ink which research has shown reduces attention. Red is best for catching the eye and ensuring greatest recall. Use red for bullet points which describe key parts of your message as well as to underline factors and figures you especially want remembered. Avoid red on points you are less concerned to emphasise.

When building to a point start by using cooler colours, such as blue or green, and work up to warmer ones, like yellow, orange and red.

Prepare most of your pages in advance so as not to

waste time having to write out a whole sheet while talking. Leave gaps for the key facts and figures to be completed during your talk.

Key words and phrases should be underlined or placed in boxes for greater clarity.

Pictures enliven your pages provided they are relevant to the message.

How to Use Flip Charts

Tape the legs of the easel to the floor to prevent it being accidentally knocked over.

If you intend changing sheets by flipping them over, adjust the stand height to make it easy. If you are tearing sheets off the pad, place one hand on the top corner of the sheet and, using the hand closest to the easel, rip the sheet carefully along its perforation, lifting it upwards slightly as you do so. This prevents unsightly ragged edges and torn sheets.

Write key points of your message lightly in pencil on the edges of the pages as an aid to memory.

Overhead Projectors (OHPs)

Advantages: Fiches can be produced quickly and easily. Printed notes can simply be photocopied onto suitable transparent sheets. In an emergency they can even be handwritten (but see note blow). The equipment is widely available, rugged and quick to set up. You do not, normally, need to darken the room. OHPs are suitable for groups of between 10 and 50 people.

Disadvantages: The fan noise from some older models can be distracting as is the glare of light on the screen when no fiche is in place.

How to Prepare OHP Fiches

It should be possible to read your fiches at a distance of six feet, when they are not on the OHP. This ensures the images will be easy to see and understand when projected.

If possible avoid handwritten fiches, which look rather amateurish and can be difficult to make out. If you are writing them by hand, convey confidence in your message by using large, thick script rather than small, thin strokes which suggest weakness.

If you intend writing points down while the fiche is being projected, pre-write them on the border then copy them out to aid your memory.

Never use more than six lines per fiche with a maximum of six words in each line.

Use both capitals and small letters as these are easier to read than a text which consists entirely of capital letters.

Never write words vertically down the fiche since this is unnatural for Western readers and makes the message harder to understand.

Choose dark colours such as red, black, blue or green rather than orange, yellow or light brown which can be more difficult to see.

Keep your chosen colours consistent throughout the message. If, for example, you decide to write headings in blue and the main text in black, continue doing so throughout the presentation.

Use different colours and type styles to highlight contrasting ideas.

Position the key points high up on the transparency for emphasis.

Two or even three transparencies can be used as overlays to build a message. If you decide to use this technique use a different colour for each fiche and spend time practising how you will lay each one down.

Write key points from your message on the card mounts to jog your memory. That way no one will notice you referring to them. Place the memory joggers so that you can read them while you are facing your audience.

How to Use OHPs

Either keep the OHP switched off until you are ready to project a fresh fiche or use a sheet of 80 gsm paper to cover the light screen until you are ready. Using paper of this thickness ensures nothing can be read in advance by your audience, but still allows you to read the next points once the projector is turned on.

Practise uncovering the transparency on cue with the content of your message.

Never remove a fiche while the OHP is turned on. The glare is distracting and the effect unprofessional.

To avoid an odd-shaped image adjust the tilt of the screen. If, for example, the top of your projected image is wider than the base, tilt the top of the screen *towards* the OHP. If the bottom of the image looks too wide and the top too narrow, move the top of the screen *away* from the projector.

Make certain the table on which your OHP is placed is stable. This avoids your audience being distracted by the image moving on the screen as you change fiches.

Use a telescope pointer to identify key points from your message on the screen rather than by pointing at the fiche. This allows you to remain facing the audience rather than standing with your back to it. It also prevents any trembling of your finger caused by anxiety to be magnified and projected for the whole audience to see.

Avoid walking through the projector beam, which is distracting and unprofessional.

Make certain there is either a back-up OHP, or at least

a spare bulb, in case the one you are using breaks down.

Slide Projectors

Advantages: Provide a high-quality image at a reasonable price. Suitable for use with large groups.
Disadvantages: The room needs to be darkened for slides to be seen clearly, especially with a large audience. Slides are also time-consuming and expensive to produce. Once a tray of slides is loaded up, you are obliged to use them in sequence and cannot vary the running order of your message to take account of changed circumstances.

How to Produce 35 mm Slides

Up to 75 per cent of the slides used in presentations are text charts. Make sure they convey information in a concise and structured manner which is easy for your audience to understand and absorb. A slide which is difficult to read distracts from your message and so reduces the overall impact of your argument. When creating text slides, keep these points in mind:

- Only introduce one idea per slide.
- Use short words and sentences.
- Write 6–8 words per line with no more than 6–8 lines per slide up to a maximum of 50 words.
- Employ the same tense throughout. Use a minimum of prepositions, adverbs and adjectives.
- Create headings which grab your audience's attention and summarise the key points of the slide.
- Avoid making slides too fancy. Excessive decoration and embellishments create a barrier to effective communication.
- When introducing statistics in support of your message

by using a visual (see below), include no more than four pieces of information per slide.

● Write headlines in both capital and lower case letters rather than capitals only since, as with OHP fiches, this makes them easier to read.

● If the slide includes an illustration, write the words below the picture rather than above it, as this speeds understanding.

How to Use Slide Projectors

Before the talk starts make certain you understand how to use the remote control. If this is attached to the projector by a cable, check it is long enough to allow you to move wherever you want.

Mark the slide 'forward' control button clearly—a piece of white tape will do—so that you do not make the mistake of suddenly going back through your slides.

If the remote operates by infra-red, ensure it changes the slides from anywhere you are likely to be standing. Although this type of remote control is sufficiently power-ful for use in even large rooms, in some positions the beam may be blocked by a pillar or drape. If the room is extremely large, the projector beam may not be strong enough to operate the projector reliably. In this case it may be possible to move the infra-red receiving device, which is attached to the projector, slightly closer to the position from which you will be speaking.

All these matters need to be checked and rehearsed *prior* to the moment you have to deliver your message, not discovered after you have started speaking.

Whenever possible stand to the right of the screen, as seen from the audience's viewpoint. This means the people in the audience, having read text slides from left to right, will naturally return their gaze to you. If you stand on the left of the screen, their eyes have to travel back across the slide to look at you, which can create subconscious antagonism and resistance to your message.

When you are to present at an unfamiliar venue, be sure to check whether the slide system available is designed for front or rear projection. Front projection means the slide projector is behind the audience and shines onto the front of the screen; with rear projection it is tucked out of sight and projects through the back of the screen. Most conferences favour back projection since it makes for a more polished and professional presentation. But it also means all your slides have to be turned around in the tray to appear the right way round from the audience's viewpoint.

It is unnerving to arrive at a venue to discover all your slides must be turned round because they have been set up for front projection. You can take a bet that as a result of time pressure at least one will end up being projected back to front, upside down or both. While not a major disaster, such a mistake detracts from the professionalism of your presentation and makes you seem less authoritative and prepared.

Always check your slides one last time as close to the moment you have to speak as possible. This will not only refresh your memory about key points in your message, but also ensure nobody has altered the running order or turned one side upside down by mistake.

If you are using the circular Kodak Carousel type slide-holder (the most widely used type), seal the tray lid in place with sticky tape. This prevents you from inadvertently tipping the contents on the floor when in a hurry and makes it less likely somebody else will accidentally change your slide order without you knowing.

When a text slide comes up on the screen during your talk, always read it to the audience. This is called 'clearing the slide' and means your audience is not distracted by reading the slide while you are continuing with your message.

When clearing the slide, make certain to maintain eye contact with your audience. Unless you know the content by heart, glance at the slide, then turn to face your listeners while giving them the line or lines. Glance back, take in another line or lines and face your audience again to speak. Never talk to the screen. Not only is this discourteous to your listeners, it also makes it harder for them to hear what you are saying since your voice is directed away from them.

Computer-Generated Slides

There are an increasing number of software packages which enable you to create presentations ranging from the quick and fairly unsophisticated to those which, while they take longer to create, offer the last word in dazzling graphics.

Widely used programs include Microsoft Power Point, Correl Draw and Harvard Graphics. Others, such as ASAP, while less sophisticated, provide a means of producing high-quality slides in the shortest possible time.
Advantages: Flexibility of production, presentation, style and output.

Images can be quickly and easily changed to take account of new information or altered demands.

The order in which the slides are presented can be changed at will, even as your presentation is being made.

With a top of the range software and hardware package virtually anything goes. You can add sound, music, animation and 'morphing', a technique much loved by television commercial directors in which one thing slowly turns into another—a sports car into a panther for instance.

Once created the slides can be printed in black and white or colour, by means of a suitable printer, and included in the hand-outs. They can also be turned into standard 35 mm slides, either in house or, more usually, by a specialist outside bureau.

Disadvantages: The initial cost is high, since the computer system needs to be fast, with a large-capacity disk drive to store memory-hungry graphics.

The learning curve with the more sophisticated packages tends to be fairly steep, although less elaborate presentation software can be mastered in just a few hours.

The main drawback is how to show the slides. With a small group, a large high-quality colour monitor may prove adequate. As your audience gets larger, however, you will need some method for projecting the slides onto a screen. This can be achieved in one of two ways.

The first is a device known as a Tablet, a colour, liquid crystal computer screen on a standard OHP which does the projection. The drawback here is that the image tends not to be very bright.

The second method is to use a computer projector which takes the image directly from your hardware system and displays it on a screen of almost any size depending on the capabilities of the projector. The problem here is one of cost, since even a fairly simple system runs into several thousands of pounds, with top of the range projectors such as the BARCO costing many times that.

One final risk is that a very elaborate and eye-catching display may distract your audience from both you and your message. They are so busy marvelling at all the special effects on show, that the reasons behind that spellbinding display of high-tech imagery pass them by.

Whether you are creating slides for 35 mm projection or use on a computer, design considerations described below still apply.

Creating and Using the Right Slides

One of the keys to reinforcing your message by means of slides is to create the right slide for the information you want to display. Let's start by looking at slides which contain mainly words.

Text Slides

There are three main types.

Title Slides: used to introduce your presentation and summarise its content.

Bullet Point Slides: for showing facts and figures in a concise and easily read format. Bullet points will help focus attention on one point in your message at a time.

They do this more effectively if the various points are displayed one at a time rather than all together on the same slide. This allows your audience to concentrate on each point in turn without being distracted by reading ahead. The technical term for slides of this type is a 'build': the message is built up over a period of time.

Table Slides: used for making comparisons, for example showing the advantages versus the disadvantages of particular proposals.

Because tables of numbers are hard to read and understand in a short space of time, it is usually better to represent numbers by means of a graph.

Graph Slides

- Omit all unnecessary detail. Supply only the figures needed to get your message across.
- Ensure graph scales are appropriate to the figures presented. If, for example, your graph lines represent a small range of numbers, such as 1 to 10, avoid a scale measuring from 0 to 100.

- Round decimals up or down to two places, i.e. 3.45678 should be shown as 3.46.

  There are five basic types of graphs:
1 **Line Graphs:** best used for showing:

- Changes across time, e.g. sales from different divisions for each quarter, as illustrated below;
- Trends;
- Large numbers of data points;
- Data as a flow rather than a series of moments.

Line Chart

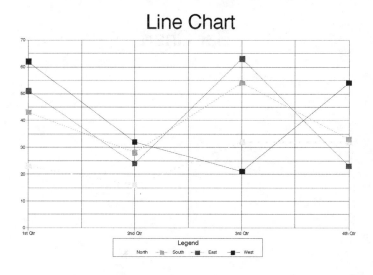

When creating line charts:

- Use no more than four lines per chart.
- Use colour to differentiate between lines, but be consistent throughout your presentation. Never change

colours halfway, e.g. sales figures shown in red on one chart and in blue on another.

● Make certain graph lines are easily distinguished from each other.
● Make lines indicating *trends* thicker than the axes.
● Make the axes thicker than grid lines.

2 Bar Graphs: used to display relative values, for example a company's sales growth over four financial quarters, as shown below. Bar charts are good for presenting statistical information because they are easier to take in at a glance.

Bar Chart

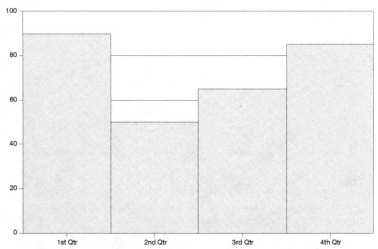

When creating bar graphs:

● Keep bar colours well differentiated. Use the same colour to represent the same set of data across all the bars.

- Employ different colours to distinguish positive and negative values.
- Restrict yourself to four bars per cluster or segments per bar. When precise values are important show these next to, or inside the top of bars.
- Never use longer bars to illustrate a lesser quantity of anything, since people tend to associate longer lines with a greater, not a lesser amount. If, for example, you wanted to compare the crime rate of different cities, using a longer bar for the location with the lowest levels of crime would give a completely mis-leading message.
- Print all labels horizontally to make them easier to read.

3 Area Charts: for displaying total quantities rather than changes within your data.

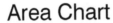

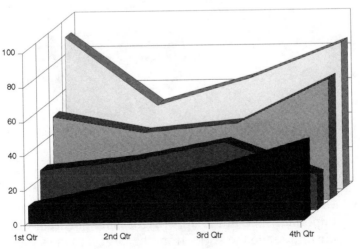

When creating area charts:

- On overlapped charts, ensure data sets with highest values are at the back. With stacked area charts, remember that the order in which data is placed will affect the chart's appearance and the message it conveys.
- Place data sets you want to emphasise at the bottom of the chart.

4 Pie Charts: used to draw attention to specific parts of the data, by means of different colours or, for greater effect, by extracting a piece of the pie as shown below.

Pie Chart

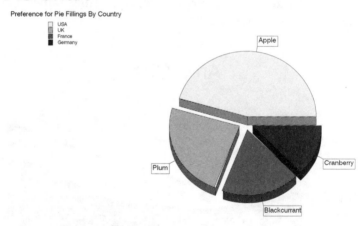

Preference for Pie Fillings By Country
USA
UK
France
Germany

Apple

Cranberry

Plum

Blackcurrant

When creating pie charts:

- Use no more than six slices. Either place the most important slice in the upper right-hand quadrant of the pie or arrange the slices from the largest to the smallest in a clockwise direction.

- Emphasise a specific slice by showing it cut from the pie, as in the illustration above.

5 Organisational Charts: for displaying relational structures, such as corporate organisation or product lines. When creating organisational charts:

- Avoid including too much information on a single chart.
- Where more than five levels of relationship exist use separate charts.
- Colour code different levels so the hierarchy is easy to understand.

Six Tips on Using Colour Correctly

1 Keep it simple! For bullet charts use no more than three colours, one for the background, one for headings and highlighting, one for the text. Only use extra colours if your slide includes corporate logos or clip-art images. As I mentioned earlier, any such decoration should be kept to a minimum and only used if you are certain it enhances your ability to get the message across.
2 Use no more than five colours for graphs.
3 Be consistent in your colour choice.
4 Make sure your colours combine legibly. Use contrasting colours for text and backgrounds.
5 A light text used against a dark background is easiest to read and looks best on 35 mm slides. For OHP fiches and hand-outs use dark text against a light background.
6 Use cooler colours (i.e. green and blue) for backgrounds and warmer ones (i.e. red and yellow) to highlight details.

Seven Tips on Choosing a Suitable Typeface

1   Sans serif fonts, such as Helvetica, are easier to read from a distance.
2   Serifed fonts, such as the Times family, are better for densely packed text such as you would use in hand-outs.
3   Avoid ornate fonts, such as Gothic Script and Letter Gothic which look arty and can be harder to read from a distance.
4   Avoid mixing fonts, either on individual charts or throughout your presentation as this looks messy and distracts attention from your message.
5   To emphasise text, use a bold, italic or underlined version of the same typeface. But do so sparingly and consistently.
6   Ensure the font is legible in the situation for which the slide is intended to be projected.
7   Use upper case sparingly as it is harder to read than a mixture of upper and lower.

CHECK THE VENUE AND EQUIPMENT PROVIDED

If you have to get your message across away from home base, there are certain checks you need to do to ensure everything runs smoothly. The more important the message the more essential it is that these are carried out in advance.

Equipment Check List

1   The proposed venue has the OHP, slide projectors, screen, monitor, video projection devices, sound amplification I need. Yes/No
2   There is a qualified technician on site to set the equip-

ment up and ensure it is working before I begin. Yes/No

3   There are sufficient power points of the appropriate size and in the right locations for the electrical equipment I shall be bringing. Yes/No

4   There are a sufficient number of stands on which to set the equipment up. Yes/No

5   The ceiling is sufficiently high for the screen to be seen from the back of the room. Yes/No

6   Nothing is hanging from the ceiling, such as a light fitting, which could block the projector beam. Yes/No

7   For 35 mm projection the room can be darkened sufficiently for the audience to see my slides easily. Yes/No

8   The picture quality of the slide projector and OHP is good. Yes/No

9   The projector lenses are clean and spare bulbs and fuses are on hand. Yes/No

10   The temperature of the room will be such as to keep my audience feeling comfortable. Yes/No

This last point is very important because it is all but impossible to communicate effectively with people shivering from cold or sweating with heat.

Setting the Stage

If you have a say in how the room is laid out, then make sure the following points are covered. Many hotel staff, even those claiming to specialise in providing conference facilities, clearly have little idea of where seats, projector and screen should be positioned in order to ensure everyone has a clear and easy view of your visual aids.

Illustrated overleaf is an example of a poorly arranged room setting. Notice that only those seated in the shaded area can see the screen well, while those to the left and right of the room will have little or no view. To make matters worse, when standing on the platform you will be blocking the view of others.

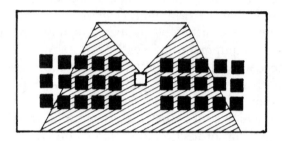

The alternative, shown below, removes some but not all of the viewing difficulties.

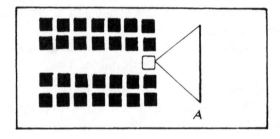

While your whole audience can, in theory, now see the screen, you will still be obstructing some people's view. Your best location is at A on the diagram. If an OHP is being used, however, you will have to walk backwards and forwards to change fiches and this is likely to prove distracting.

Where the room is long and narrow, you may need to bring in a larger screen so that those seated towards the back can see without straining. Avoid this problem by following the 6 rule. This states that 'The distance from screen to the most distant member of the audience should be no greater than the width of the screen multiplied by six.' In other words, if the room is 30 feet long, you will need a screen at least five feet wide to ensure those at the back can see your slides comfortably.

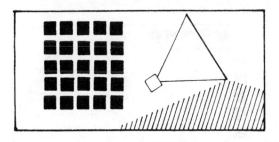

The illustration above shows the best position for the screen, given the same room lay-out. By placing it in one corner you ensure everyone in the audience has a good view and you can move anywhere in the cross-hatched area without obstructing it.

In different situations you may choose to use one of the variations shown below.

Centre Table

Sometimes the small room size makes this the only option available to you. Such a lay-out should be avoided when there are more than twelve in your audience.

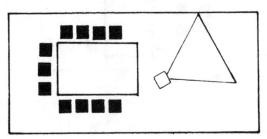

Horseshoe or U-Shaped

Use with any audience of less than 30. It encourages discussion and participation among participants.

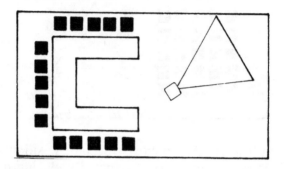

Office Meeting

The best choice for a small meeting where you are unable to book a room with a conference table. For such a small group it would be better to dispense with the projector and work on a flip chart.

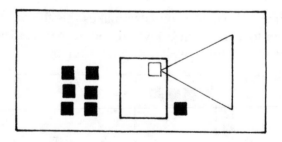

Classroom

Useful when there are too many participants to be fitted into a U-shape design. When booking a hotel room check the number of people it can hold in either a classroom or theatre (minus tables) arrangement.

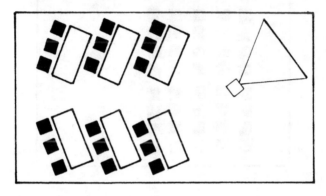

While many speakers dislike tables, seeing them as an obstacle to getting close to their audiences, most participants appreciate having a solid surface on which to write, a place for notes, a glass of water, etc.

The chevron style illustrated above provides for a wider centre aisle and enables those attending to see one another more easily.

Theatre or Auditorium Style

Although far from ideal, you may not have any other choice when the group is large. Make sure the screen is large enough for all those present to have a good view.

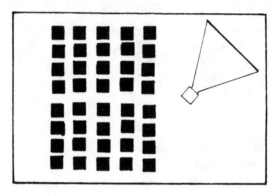

Amphitheatre

Provides for the maximum number of people all of whom have an excellent view of the screen.

The seats are ranked, with each row being slightly higher than the next. Because they are usually fixed in place,

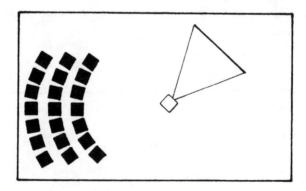

breaking participants into smaller groups for discussions, brain-storming and team exercises is far more difficult. When you are offered such an arrangement and syndicate work is required, hire smaller rooms in which the teams can do their work.

CHAPTER 12

Getting Your Message Across Without Saying a Word

To others we are not ourselves but a performer in their lives
cast for a part we do not even know that we are playing.
Elizabeth Bibesco, *Haven*

The owner of a pony was determined to have it trained
using only kindness. After much searching he found a
horse trainer with a reputation for great gentleness. On
their first meeting the owner was horrified when the man
smacked his startled pony hard on the flanks.

'I was told you only used kindness when training
horses,' he protested angrily.

'I do' agreed the man. 'But first you have to attract their
attention!'

It's the same when getting your message across: in order to persuade an audience to listen, you must first catch its attention.

This is done not so much by what you say as by what you do not say—at least with your mouth. At a first meeting important messages are conveyed via your dress and deportment, your gestures, stance, posture and expression.

Research suggests that we obtain around 75 per cent of information about other people from their body language, 15 per cent from their tone of voice and only 10 per cent from the words they use.

While I believe the extent to which we are influenced by non-verbal messages varies according to the circumstances of the encounter, there is no doubt that what we see often influences us far more than what we hear. An excellent example of this is the 1960 television debate between the two US presidential candidates, Richard Milhous Nixon and John F. Kennedy. Before that first debate Nixon had been leading the race and was being confidently tipped as the next incumbent of the White House. All that changed in the brief time the debate lasted.

Exhausted from the campaign trail and still recovering from an illness, he arrived at the studios late and refused make-up. While Kennedy came across as boyish, charismatic and open, Nixon, sweating and pallid, looked like the loser he was about to become.

Radio audiences, who heard only the arguments, voted by a majority that Nixon had won the debate. Television viewers, more influenced by the images on their screens than the words emerging from their loudspeakers, voted Kennedy the winner. It was enough to make him president by a tiny margin.

These days, of course, an army of spin doctors, PR consultants, image specialists and make-up artists would never allow a politician to be placed in such a position.

As you lack those legions of highly paid experts, it is up to you to ensure nothing of the sort ever happens to you.

The techniques required are called Impression Management. That is communicating the kind of message you want to get across, not just with your mouth but by using every aspect of your being to maximum advantage.

The Importance of First Impressions

How long do you have to manage a first impression? Studies suggest no more than four minutes.

'That first meeting is the key meeting. Clients instantly assess you when you walk through the door,' claims Basil Towers, chairman and managing director of Christow Consultants. 'It all comes down to chemistry—whether the client thinks he or she can work with you.'

While it may not be entirely correct to say that nobody ever gets 'a second chance to make a first impression', it is certainly true that a bad first impression can be hard to overcome. Having made up their minds, people tend to be reluctant to change them, preferring to ignore or dismiss any new information which might contradict their original assessment.

THE ART OF IMPRESSION MANAGEMENT

To match the impression you create to the expectations of those to whom you are seeking to get your message across you need to respond promptly and sensitively to the demands of each audience.

Unless you are an eccentric known and loved for your unique way of dressing, my advice is always to choose a formal and conservative look. This is especially true when communicating in a corporate arena. Business people tend to be suspicious of those who dress in an unfamiliar or outlandish manner. As a result they will be more wary and much less receptive to your views.

You will find it far easier to get your message across if your listeners feel comfortable and relaxed. This is more likely if the unspoken message being conveyed by your clothes, grooming and manner encourages trust, belief and confidence.

Always seek to blend with your surroundings as much as possible, while, at the same time, appearing in some way noticeable and memorable. You can achieve this while following the prevailing dress code by 'dressing up' some-what in terms of clothes and grooming.

Clearly the style and dress most suitable for getting your message across to one group could prove inappropriate for others.

In the days when I was a university lecturer, it was occasionally necessary for me to lecture in a suit and tie because I had to go on to another, more formal, appoint-ment immediately after. I remember feeling awkward and out of place when faced with rows of casually dressed students. But I would have felt even more uncomfortable if I had turned up for a meeting with high-ranking business executives dressed in blue jeans and a T-shirt!

If in doubt the best advice is to play safe.

Most audiences expect and appreciate speakers who dress neatly and rather formally. By lending you an air of authority this makes your message more believable and acceptable. A grey or dark blue business suit with a plain shirt or blouse conveys a sense of professionalism.

Men should avoid bold stripes on either shirts or ties, as these prove distracting. Afterwards your audience may remember nothing more about your message than the eye-catching pattern of your tie. For men, black shoes with plain socks are safest.

Once you have started your talk it's perfectly acceptable,

even desirable in some situations, to dispense with some formality by taking off your jacket or loosening your tie, for instance. When done dramatically, for example by tossing your jacket across a chair, these touches of theatre convey an intense, informal, shirt-sleeves attitude which greatly impresses some audiences.

Peter Bingle, managing director of Westminster Strategy, describes how when his team is well underway with a message,

> Off come the jackets and you try to involve people immediately. We do that to overcome the formality of the occasion and make it as relaxed as possible. If we go in with three pin-stripe suits on our side and three on theirs, it's very difficult to get some humour and an informal atmosphere going.

Remember clothes are not simply your *covering*, they also play a crucial role in the way you communicate.

Check Your Grooming Too

In corporate settings, make sure your hair is trim, clean and (if you are a man) not overly long.

Clean-shaven men must ensure their shave is a close one. Five o'clock shadow communicates a slightly disreputable message at any hour, but particularly at nine in the morning! If you have a beard, this should be trim and not too extravagant. Bear in mind also that research has shown many people either consciously or subconsciously mistrust bearded men. They are frequently perceived as radical, left-wing and potentially subversive. As a result the value of their messages is often discounted. There is an unwritten rule, for example, that no news reader for BBC television should ever have a beard.

Your hands must be clean with the fingernails neatly trimmed and free from dirt.

Jewellery, apart from a wedding ring, is best avoided by men while women should not wear anything flashy. At best it may prove distracting, and you could suggest you are less than professional.

Remove anything from your pockets, such as a balled-up handkerchief, spectacle case, wad of notes, which spoils the line of your clothes.

Get rid too of anything likely to make a noise, such as a pocketful of loose change or jangling jewellery.

If you are seeking to get your message across at a major conference, where you will be standing in front of a large audience on a well-lit stage, some make-up, for men as well as women, may be in order.

It's not so long since businessmen would run a mile before letting make-up artists get their powder puffs on them. They looked on any embellishments to their 'natural' appearance as needlessly theatrical at best and effeminate at worst. These days most executives have woken up to the fact that appearing pale-faced and sweaty before your workforce is not the best way to stay at the top.

All you usually need is a little face powder to cover any blemishes and keep you from sweating under the lights. If this seems a little too daring for your taste, then get a tan, either by holidaying in the sun or, even better and far more safely, by applying a tanning agent which works in the absence of sunlight.

While these may seem trivial points to you, always remember that clothes and other aspects of your appearance are an essential part of the message you are trying to get across.

Research clearly shows that how people look plays a major role in how others make up their minds about them. Of course this is illogical, but many of our judgements stem from equally irrational assumptions, such as the idea that all blondes are dumb and everybody who wears glasses has above average intelligence.

Checking Your Own Silent Speech

Some professional speakers suggest using a video to record and check your performance when rehearsing before an important presentation. The main problem is that, however you frame the picture, the camera will observe you in a way your audience does not.

If it is focused on your face so you can analyse your expressions, for example, the close-ups will be markedly different from how your listeners, seated at a distance, will see you. Your facial expressions will be exaggerated in a way that will not occur during the presentation.

Your audience will be looking at your entire body, which means posture and stance are equally important when getting your message across. Yet a camera placed far enough away to record these details is going to produce a screen image so small it will be hard to see anything at all.

For these reasons I prefer a full-length mirror which shows everything your audience will see.

It is even better to do a final rehearsal before an audience of friends, relatives or colleagues. Ask them to provide constructive comments on content and verbal and non-verbal delivery.

Use the check list below to provide consistent feedback when rehearsing before a small group of people.

Body Language Check List

Ask your rehearsal audience to tick as appropriate.

Gestures:
a   Too few, made presentation seem awkward and 'wooden';

b   Just right, helped flow of words;
c   Too many, looked fidgety and messy.

Posture:
a   Too stiff, looked like sentry on parade;
b   Just right, appeared relaxed yet positive;
c   Too relaxed, looked uninterested.

Expression:
a   Face was rather immobile, seemed ill-at-ease;
b   Appeared relaxed and at ease;
c   Too animated, tried too hard to look enthusiastic.

Eye Contact:
a   Insufficient, felt ignored and left out;
b   Gave eye contact to whole audience;
c   Felt threatened, gazed at me often and at length.

Overall:
a   Anxious and lacking confidence;
b   Comfortable, relaxed and confident;
c   Seemed rather too aggressive.

READY, STEADY, GO . . .

In Chapter Nine I used a space-shuttle analogy to divide the act of getting your message across into three elements: the launch, the mission, the safe landing. There we were concerned with the verbal content of getting your message across. Now let's explore the rules governing its silent speech components in the same context.

The Launch

Here are eight rules to observe during the launch of your presentation:

1 When you come into the room walk like a winner. We tell a great deal from the way people move around, as George Orwell describes in *Down and Out in Paris and London*:

> There was something in his drifting style of walk, and the way he had of hunching his shoulders forward, essentially abject. Seeing him walk, you felt instinctively that he would sooner take a blow than give one.

So move calmly, coolly and deliberately. Without appearing apprehensive or lacking in enthusiasm, take your time entering the room. Hurrying not only communicates nervousness; it also robs you of some authority and status. Who runs the most in offices? The juniors scurrying to deliver messages, fetch coffee, post letters and take out the trash. Never allow yourself to be confused with an office junior by seeming in too much of a hurry. Show in the way you walk your confidence in yourself and the message you have come to deliver.

There's another benefit from proceeding with a measured pace. Going faster increases physical arousal, so making you more anxious. We run *because* we are afraid, but we also become more fearful *because* we are running. So always walk confidently and walk tall. Move purposefully like somebody comfortable and confident with the message he or she is to deliver.

2 When addressing even a small group, always stand up

to speak if this is at all possible. Audiences pay greater attention to speakers who are standing.

Giving yourself that additional height serves two important purposes. First it helps *you* feel more confident and assertive. Secondly, it communicates greater authority to your seated listeners. This is because we look up, physically and mentally, to people taller than ourselves. They are perceived as enjoying greater power, confidence and mastery than shorter folk. Until Jimmy Carter came along, for example, the taller of the two principal US presidential candidates had always won the race.

When we were children, all those around us with power and authority over our lives were adults who towered above us. Now, even as grown-ups, we tend to carry these subconscious feelings of vague inferiority to tall people. Incidentally this is also why speakers who address an audience from a conference stage or podium are usually seen as more imposing than those who speak the same words from floor level.

On some occasions you may need to find an excuse for getting up out of your chair, such as passing around hand-outs or writing on a flip chart.

3   Pause before you start to speak and look around your audience, smiling as you do so. Make brief eye contact with several individuals. When addressing a large group, make certain your initial gaze takes in not only those seated directly in front of you, but people at the sides and back of the room as well. This gives them a chance to tune into you before your message is launched. It also allows you to get those last few butterflies flying in formation.

If you feel anxious, try to find a member of the group who appears attentive and friendly, then deliver your opening remarks primarily to that person. But do not gaze at them for too long or not only will everybody else in your audience start feeling left out, but the person being stared at so relentlessly will begin to feel distinctly uncomfortable and threatened. Before very long his or her friendly expression will turn to one of discomfort or even alarm!

4   'Plant' yourself before the audience by ensuring your weight is distributed equally between both feet, with your legs slightly apart and soles flat on the ground.

Your posture should be vertical, to ensure a smooth and easy flow of air into the lungs, but relaxed. There must be nothing ramrod about your stance since needless muscle tensions will increase your anxiety and tense up your throat.

Pay special attention to your head and shoulders. The head should be level, to smooth out your throat and allow the larynx to function efficiently. Your shoulders must be relaxed, as tension here will change the quality of your voice, making it sound equally tense.

If you doubt this, try speaking a few words right now with your shoulders loose and relaxed. Now repeat those words having first tensed your shoulders by pulling them sharply back. Notice how relaxed and conversational your voice is in the first position and how forced and unnatural the words sound in the second.

5   While speaking, make sure everybody in your audience receives eye contact at some time.

Hold your gaze on either a single person, or a small group of people when addressing a large audience, for around five seconds before moving on. Let your gaze cover everyone present, even those seated at the back of the room.

If you ever get a chance to watch an old-time theatre artist at work, notice how he makes certain every single member of the audience is made to feel the songs or jokes are being directed at him or her alone. Nobody is allowed to feel neglected, whether sitting in the stalls, the boxes, the balcony or high up in the gallery.

One of the single most common mistakes made by speakers is to direct their gaze either at the rear wall or the floor or the ceiling or the projection screen.

When brief eye contact *is* made, it is usually confined to a few people in the centre of the front row, with everybody else present being turned into 'non people' through the absence of eye contact.

Failing to engage with every single person present on several occasions during your presentation creates two barriers to effective communication:

- Those denied eye contact feel less involved with your message, and consequently less persuaded by it, than those to whom you do give eye contact. Remember you want to get your message across to everyone present, not just a randomly favoured few.
- By not directing your gaze at members of an audience you are failing to point your mouth at them either. Your words will be absorbed by the walls, the ceiling, the floor or the projection screen, making it harder for people to hear.

6 Be aware of what you are doing with your hands. This is one of the biggest problems facing inexperienced speakers when they are not pointing, gesturing or displaying props.

The safest places to put your hands are behind your back or at your side. Never stick them in your pockets, which looks slovenly, or constantly fidget with them, as this is not only distracting but also betrays anxiety.

If you are a natural gesticulator—as I am—do not

feel embarrassed about waving your hands around to illustrate points. Provided this is not done to an absurd extent, turning you into a kind of talking windmill, gestures convey a sense of energy, excitement and enthusiasm.

7   Always begin on an upbeat note. People far prefer listening to a positive speaker who sounds as if she knows how to get things done, than someone coming across as bored, apathetic and generally uninterested in the subject.

8   Paint word pictures so that listeners not only hear but 'see' your message unfolding before them. Use phrases such as: 'What would you do if . . .', 'Assume you are . . .', 'Imagine you have just . . .'

The Mission

Once you are under way, the crucial elements you must convey in order to get your message across are competence, knowledge and enthusiasm. The first two depend on your knowledge of the subject plus the special preparation you undertook when putting the message together.

Enthusiasm arises from your whole outlook on life. It is probably the single most important ingredient in any communication.

I stressed its importance in Chapter Four but make no apology for returning to it now. There is no great communicator in the world, from Billy Graham to Martin Luther King, from John F. Kennedy to Winston Churchill, who has not possessed this quality to the nth degree.

In the words of B. C. Forbes, millionaire businessman and founder of *Forbes* magazine:

Enthusiasm is the all-essential human jet propeller. White heat enthusiasm can melt the hardest problems

... It begets boldness, courage, kindles confidence, overcomes doubts, creates energy, the source of all accomplishment.

Enthusiasm is joyous excitement, a burning desire to get your message across which will be sparked only by a genuine belief both in yourself and in the message you are communicating. Only the truly persuaded can ever hope to persuade.

Convey that enthusiasm both verbally and with your body language in the following manner. I term it the ABC approach to selling excitement.

A Animation. More than a century ago, psychologist William James emphasised the fact that how we behave and how we feel are closely related. Smile and you will feel happier. Cry and your mood will become more depressed. Move faster and your anxiety rises. Slow down and your fears will also subside.

B Believe in your message. You can only get across a message to somebody else once you have taken it on board yourself.

C Create excitement and confidence in yourself while speaking by fixing a successful outcome firmly in your mind.

These six rules of navigation will help you steer your mission from the launch pad to the safe landing.

1 Pace yourself. Go neither too fast, so that you risk starting to gabble, nor too slowly, so that your voice becomes a drone.

Change gear like a motorist driving in variable conditions, speeding up on some sections and slowing down on those parts of the 'journey' where it is essential that your audience clearly understands and remembers key ideas from your message.

2   Appear animated but avoid striding. I have seen some speakers pace the platform like caged tigers, forcing their listeners to flick their gaze first left and then right and then left again, just as if they were tennis spectators.

All movements should be deliberate and precise or they come across as anxious and distracting fidgets.

3   If you are using objects to demonstrate points, wherever possible hold them up so that everyone in the room can see them. Pick them up using the hand closest to the table on which the props have been placed. Avoid reaching across your body with the opposite arm, since this will oblige you to turn away from your listeners.

4   Use pauses to emphasise points and allow your audience to reflect on what you have just said.

Never be afraid of silences. They seem to last far longer to you than to those listening to you. Practise standing before a group and keeping quiet for several seconds. When doing this, however, be sure to continue giving your listeners ample eye contact.

5   If anything goes wrong, never let the audience know unless it becomes absolutely essential. Remember that your listeners only get what you give them.

If a slide is projected out of sequence but it is possible to change your message slightly to take this slip into account, smoothly alter the communication without letting on what has happened.

Only let on that all is not as it should be when you are given no other choice in the matter. At this point apologise, explain, rectify and move on.

Never make a big deal out of a small mistake or

your audience may remember the blunder better than your message.

6   When presenting a controversial message, adopt the following strategy for securing agreement most quickly and easily. If your audience

- Already favours your proposals
- Lacks in-depth knowledge of the subject
- Is unlikely to be exposed to counter arguments,

give only one side—your side—of the argument. Avoid arousing doubts and concerns where none already exist.

If, however, your listeners

- Oppose your proposals
- Know as much as or more than you do about the subject
- Will be exposed to contrary viewpoints,

you must fairly and clearly present both sides of the argument, while also explaining the reasoning which led you to adopt a particular view of the matter. If you are open in this way your message will come across as more, rather than less credible and trustworthy.

The Safe Touchdown

Your mission accomplished, all that remains is to return safely to earth and make sure your passengers carry away a positive final impression of both you and your message.

Remember that the primacy and recency effects described earlier in the book mean that how you leave them feeling is every bit as crucial to success as how you started them out feeling.

1   Finish, do not just stop. I have seen speakers ruin the effect of a well-presented message by simply stumbling

to the close. 'Er . . . well . . . I guess that's all I really wanted to say' impresses no one.

As well as presenting the right verbal conclusions, as discussed in Chapter Nine, make sure your body language also communicates a firm 'The End' before you sit down or leave the platform.

2 Know when to stop. When you are speaking off the cuff to a small group it is essential not to carry on past the point where you have got your message across. Fall into this trap and, as I explained earlier, you risk talking your listeners out of your proposals just as effectively as they were talked into them.

Judging when enough has been said comes with practice, but you can avoid mistakes by becoming aware of the body language people use when 'sold' on your ideas. Professional salespeople call such non-verbal signals 'buy signs'. They become easy to spot once you know what to watch out for.

People give three key silent speech signals which help you to identify the moment you have succeeded in getting your message across.

- They become more relaxed. As people come around to your way of thinking they usually become more relaxed. Watch especially for the release of tensions in the back, the shoulders and the face muscles.
- They move closer to you. People persuaded by your message will often lean towards you in their seats, while those still unconvinced are likely to lean away.
- They offer you greater eye contact. Once persuaded, listeners in a small group will return eye contact more frequently and more readily.

3 Finish with eye contact around the audience to let everyone leave with the impression your message holds a special relevance for him or her personally.

4 If you feel comfortable doing so, 'open' yourself physically by raising and extending your arms. Such an expansive gesture conveys the impression of emotional and intellectual 'openness' and so increases trust in your message.

5 When you have been talking to a large audience, never dash off the platform. Even if there is no applause, pause for a moment or two at the end of both your main message and any question and answer session which follows. If there *is* applause, acknowledge it by smiling and looking around the room.

6 When leaving the platform move purposefully so that the confidence and authority generated by your message is not diminished by what looks like a hasty retreat.

Establishing Intimacy Within a Small Group

Avoid having seats in rows like a classroom. Depending on the size of the group and the space available, create a more informal seating plan, such as a horseshoe shape. But also avoid placing your audience in a circle around you, which makes it far harder to give effective eye contact to everybody in the group. You either end up trying to communicate with a number of listeners through your back, or else start spinning like a top to let everyone have a chance of communicating with you face to face.

Develop a memory for names so that you can refer to members of a small group by their names from the start. Better yet, make a discreet note as you ask them their names right at the start. I am a greater believer in the Chinese saying that the 'palest ink is better than the best memory'.

Name cards placed in front of each member of the group are also useful on occasions, especially when they are strangers to each other and you want to encourage open discussion of the points raised in your message.

Use an even more conversational verbal and non-verbal style than you would with a larger group.

Getting Your Message Across in One-to-One Settings

So far I have looked at some of the keys to successful communication when talking to groups of various sizes. But there will be many occasions when you want to get your message across to just one other person.

Understanding the psychology of office lay-outs will help you decide where it is best to position yourself for each type of meeting This is no trivial matter since evidence shows your choice exerts a powerful influence over your ability to communicate effectively.

One of the earliest studies, by Dr Robert Sommer,[1] looked at conversations between people sitting around a cafeteria table (see illustration opposite).

Dr Sommer found that those sitting in positions F and A were twice as likely to talk to each other as those at C and B, while they in turn were three times more likely to chat than people at C and D. No conversations were recorded for the remaining positions.

When your message is confrontational choose a face-to-face position. If you want to win someone's co-operation a right-angle location is far more effective.

Sitting directly opposite someone, especially across a desk, creates subconscious feelings of confrontation which

1 Robert Sommer and Barbara A. Sommer, 'Social facilitation effects in coffeehouses', *Environment and Behaviour*, vol. 21, no. 6, pp. 651–66, November 1989.

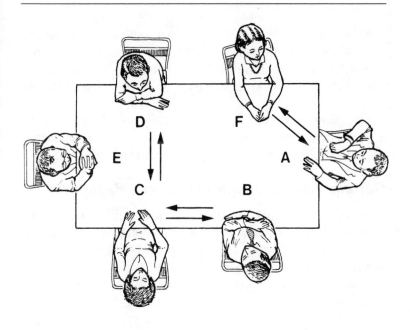

may reduce your chances of agreement. This applies particularly when one man is talking to another.

If a third party, such as a specialist, who is hostile to your message is present, try to arrange it so that he sits opposite his employer while you sit at right angles to both of them. This ensures the client is less receptive to negative comments.

A man communicating with a woman should always try to sit at right angles to her rather than beside her, since this implies an intimacy which may create annoyance or apprehension.

If offered a chair significantly lower than that occupied by the other person decline it politely where there is an alternative, since being lower puts you at a psychological disadvantage and means your message is likely to convey less authority and confidence.

Where possible, select a seat without armrests, which will allow you greater freedom for gesturing, and one which lets you sit upright. This means you will appear as tall as possible, making it easier to control the available space.

Selecting your seat may also enable you to move it to a more favourable position. This could be out of direct sunlight or into a better orientation with the other person.

Getting Your Message Across in a Restaurant

Reserve a table close to the wall, preferably in a corner location. If you sit at a table in the centre of a restaurant you will be distracted by other diners and waiters constantly passing around you. Take the corner seat for yourself since this gives you an excellent view of all that is going on.

No matter whether your guest faces you or sits at right angles, *you* will still occupy most of his or her field of vision. What is more, because the restaurant wall or walls provide you with a more neutral background than the busy restaurant, your non-verbal messages will be easy to see and therefore more powerful.

Only when there is no alternative should you sit side by side, since body-language signals are difficult to observe in such a position.

Handling Objections Non-Verbally

In Chapter Eight I discussed ways of dealing verbally with objections to your message. But how you use your body is equally important in bringing the situation back under control.

As soon as an objection is raised, use your body language to communicate assertiveness. You can do this by turning slightly away from the person raising the objection, leaning back in your seat and allowing one arm to rest over the back of the chair. A man can also cross his legs.

When all the objections have been raised and rephrased, as described in Chapter Eight, convey your readiness to co-operate by uncrossing your legs, leaning forward and turning your shoulders towards the person who raised the objection while using your hands to illustrate various points.

Avoid eye contact with the objector to make it more difficult for him or her to interrupt you.

Whenever possible, increase co-operation by arranging the chairs so that you are *beside* the individual most likely to object.

Using the Power Lift

This powerful piece of body language enables you to control which part of your message is remembered best. It works most successfully when speaking one to one but can also be used with a small group.

Here's what you do. When you reach a part of the message you especially want to get across and ensure your audience recalls it more easily than anything else you have said, simply raise your right hand towards your right eye (if you are left-handed you can equally well do this with your left hand and left eye). You will find this compels your listener(s) to follow your moving hand and obliges them to make eye contact with you. Hence its name.

Once you have compelled the other person(s) to look you in the eyes, you simply repeat the key part of your message. Days later, when perhaps the bulk of what you said to them has been forgotten, this part of the communication will remain crystal clear in their minds! Try it and see for yourself.

213

CHAPTER 13

Getting Your Message Across at Meetings

The camel—a horse designed by a committee.

Anon

Meetings can be productive exchanges of views or black holes into which time, effort and energy vanish without trace. The one thing almost all of them share is a potential for getting their business done with far greater efficiency if only those involved knew how to communicate better.

While some people who attend meetings make useful suggestions and listen carefully to the views of others, many more seem less concerned with getting their messages across than with playing office politics.

Here are six ways to combat the bores and communicate more effectively the next time you attend, or chair, a meeting. These can be used in addition to the more general points described earlier in the book.

Rule 1: Know What You are Talking About

Communications can break down at any time, before, during and even after the meeting. Failure to clarify the issues to be discussed during the meeting results in confusion, time-wasting, lost opportunities and frustration all round.

When ideas and decisions arrived at during the meeting are not communicated effectively to those involved, unnecessary actions may be taken and necessary ones not be put into practice.

So before attending any meeting make absolutely certain you understand the reason(s) why it is being called and the topics to be discussed. If you need additional information, make certain you do your homework in advance. Ensure you have all the relevant documents and are fully briefed on what is to be discussed.

Getting across the wrong message or one which is even slightly off target is obviously a waste of everyone's time. As Peter Drucker puts it: 'Efficiency is doing the thing right, but effectiveness is doing the right thing.' The only way you can be sure of 'doing the right thing' is by careful planning and preparation.

If you are responsible for holding and running the meeting, then be sure to set clear goals. Start by asking yourself: What purpose is be served by holding this meeting? Is it to:

- Make a decision?
- Analyse or solve a problem?
- Provide new information?
- Collect information about a particular project?

Know in your own mind what outcome you are aiming to

215

achieve and communicate that goal to the others who will be attending. Prepare a one-line mission statement and place it in clear view of all those at the meeting.

Rule 2: Insist on a Written Agenda

No matter how brief the meeting, insist on, or provide, a written agenda and have this circulated in advance. If you are chairing the meeting you will have no problem in arranging this. When someone else is in charge, request an agenda or offer to prepare it yourself and have it circulated as much in advance of the meeting as is realistic. This will give all those attending sufficient time for preparation, significantly reducing the risk of confusions and communication breakdowns.

Without such an agenda, meetings frequently deteriorate into general, unfocused debates and miss out on key issues.

When organising a meeting, ask yourself what you want those attending to gain from it. What changes are you seeking in the way they feel or behave?

Rule 3: Restrict Invitations to Meetings

Whenever practicable, only attend a meeting if you really have to be there. Know why you are going and, when making a contribution, what message you will be getting across.

When you are running the meeting, only invite those who absolutely need to be there. The more people there are the harder it will be for you or anyone else to get your messages across successfully.

If you have any choice in the matter, check the value of the meeting as you would any other time-consuming task. Ask yourself:

● Why am I proposing to attend this meeting?

- What am I likely to get from it that will help me do my job more efficiently?

Rule 4: Sustain Interest

As I explained in Chapter Two, the WIIFM factor means people will only pay close attention to messages which have personal relevance. To get your message across at a meeting, make certain you are addressing this communications need to the full.

When running a meeting, vary the format, pace and style. Prevent dominant speakers from taking over the meeting. If two lock horns and start discussing an issue between themselves, ignoring the others who are present, reschedule it as a meeting between those two protagonists.

Much time is wasted when people fail to listen with sufficient care to what is being said. As a result, points are raised after they have already been discussed, and questions asked to which answers have already been provided. Use the positive listening techniques described in Chapter Three to ensure that all your messages to the meeting address central issues and are not merely an excuse to demonstrate your own wit or wisdom.

Rule 5: Keep Your Messages Brief

Say what you want to say and stop. Avoid the temptation to ramble on.

Never interrupt another speaker, no matter how strongly you disagree with what he or she is saying. Allowing her to finish before expressing any views of your own is not simply a question of politeness, it's also the best way of making certain your message gets priority. This is because by allowing her to finish without interruption you:

- Ensure all the strengths and weaknesses of her view-

point are out in the open. If interrupted, she may counter your objection by simply going on with her original
argument, perhaps prefaced by a sarcastic: 'If only you
had let me finish, you would have found out that . . .'
- Make it harder for her to counter your own objections,
since most if not all of her ammunition will have been
used up.
- Strengthen your own hand, since you will come across
to the rest of the group as somebody who has listened
carefully to the opposing arguments and weighed up
the pros and cons carefully before raising any
objection.

Avoid personal attacks which are disruptive and unpro-
ductive. They waste time by forcing those attacked either
to defend themselves or to launch a counter-offensive.

By raising the emotional temperature of the meeting
they distract others from thinking clearly about your ideas
and so lessen your chances of getting your message across
successfully.

Rule 6: Conclude with a Plan of Action

Whether as a participant or chairperson, encourage those
present to formulate a clear plan of action as a result of
the meeting. If you are in charge, make it clear to everyone
that you will be following up on what has been agreed.
Where a decision has been taken which affects you, always
act on it.

CHAPTER 14

Getting Your Message Across by Phone

The far is near. Our feeblest whispers fly
Where cannon falter, thunders faint and die.
Your little song the telephone can float
As free as fetters are the bluebird's note . . .
The miles are minutes and the minutes breaths . . .
    Benjamin Franklin Taylor, 'The Wonder of Forty Years'

On 10 March, 1876, in a Boston boarding-house, a 29-year-old Scots-born teacher of the deaf named Alexander Graham Bell achieved the world's first intelligible transmission of speech using electricity.

His historic words—'Mr Watson, come here, I want you'—have been interpreted as either an order (he addressed his assistant in this formal manner) or a cry for help. Alexander Graham Bell had just spilt battery acid all over his trousers.

219

Remarkably, in view of its overwhelming importance to modern society, the telephone gained acceptance only slowly, with many businessmen sceptical of the new device. The President of Western Union turned down an offer to buy all rights for $100,000 with the sneering comment: 'What use could this company make of an electric toy?'

It took a hundred years for Bell's telephone system to develop into the largest and most sophisticated network ever constructed by man. Today there are more than 700 million phones.

For such an intensely complex system, its operation for the user is remarkably simple. Yet this very simplicity can create a barrier to getting your message across. For the telephone's ease of use disguises the fact that you need to learn how to use it well.

The rewards from doing so are, however, considerable. Knowing how to get your messages across by telephone can help reduce workplace stress, increase efficiency and give you the winning edge in an increasingly competitive business environment.

TAKING CONTROL, KEEPING CONTROL

The secret of getting your message across over the phone is to stay in control of:

- Your emotions;
- The nature of the call.

Emotional Control

As physical tension increases, your concentration starts to slip and your ability to communicate effectively declines. As I explained earlier, excess tension in the muscles of the face, neck and shoulders also changes the way you sound over the phone. A tense man sounds elderly, irritable and inflexible, while a tense woman is likely to be judged as emotional and irrational.

Banish tension by relaxing mind and muscles prior to making a challenging call. Here's how to unwind quickly and discreetly while still seated at your desk.

- Deliberately tighten your muscles. Clench fists, curl toes, stretch legs, flatten your stomach and take a deep breath. Hold for a slow count to five.
- Breathe out slowly. Let your body go limp. Drop the shoulders, unclench your fingers, flop into the chair.
- Take another deep breath. Hold for five seconds. While breathing out make sure your teeth are unclenched.
- Breathe quietly for a further five seconds. Feel a deep calm and relaxation flowing through your whole body.
- Finally soothe jangled nerves by picturing yourself lying on the golden sand of a sun-warmed beach by a clear blue ocean. Hold this image for a few moments.

Banish Microphone Fright

One reason some people find it harder to get their message across over the telephone than in face-to-face encounters is microphone fright. As I shall explain in the next chapter, even the brightest and normally most articulate of men and women can find themselves lost for words when asked to make a live radio or television broadcast.

Speaking over the telephone can have the same effect. You can banish this fear by never trying to talk *at* the handset. Instead, imagine the person you are calling is sitting opposite you and speak to him or her directly. Picture the person's responses to your remarks. See him or her smiling at your witticisms or beaming with pleasure as you offer a compliment.

If you know what the other person looks like, having a

picture in your mind should not be too hard. Some people find it helpful to place a photograph on the desk and to chat to that.

When talking to strangers, try to create mental pictures from their tones of voice. If they are deep and sonorous, they probably have a big build. Light and hesitant tones are more likely to indicate slightly built, somewhat diffident speakers.

While speaking over the phone use exactly the same body language as you would when meeting someone. If it's a normal part of your communications style to use gesture and plenty of facial expression, do the same on the phone. Reflecting the way you feel in your facial muscles makes your voice sound far more relaxed, confident and natural.

Controlling the Nature of Your Calls

Make the call yourself whenever possible. This places you at a psychological advantage over the person receiving the call, for three reasons:

- *You* have decided to take up that person's time and he or she has submitted to this request. By accepting your call, therefore, the other person is allowing him- or herself to be, at least temporarily, dominated by you.
- *You* can choose how to start the conversation and have a better chance of directing it along the most advantageous lines.
- By making the call you are in a better position to end it without causing offence, once you have got your message across.

Have a Clear Message in Mind

Before dialling have a clear idea of what you hope your message will achieve. Ask yourself: 'What is my purpose in making this call?'

If you are trying to fix an appointment and anticipate refusal, have several possible times and dates in mind. By asking, 'Is ten o'clock on Friday 23rd convenient?' you focus the other's attention on whether she is free at that time and date instead of wondering why she should see you in the first place.

Delay the Call Until Your Message is Fully Prepared

Delay, usually a time-waster, often proves a face-saver under these circumstances:

- When you are very angry, or upset in some other way. Delaying the call allows you to calm down and so get your message across clearly, calmly and effectively.
- When you feel too tired to get your message across successfully. Wait until you feel rested and better able to cope with the call.
- When it is essential for you to be certain of your facts, for instance if making a complaint. Having all the details to hand before dialling makes it less likely you will get confused and allow yourself to be side-tracked.

Make Your Message More Authoritative

Do this by standing while telephoning. This will, literally, heighten your sense of authority while sharpening your mind. When we stand up, our whole system becomes more physically and mentally alert.

223

Change Your Ear to Change Your Understanding

If the call requires you to analyse complicated facts and figures, or to review information in a logical, objective manner, try putting the handset to your right ear.

Sounds arriving in this ear will arrive at the left side of your brain slightly ahead of those travelling to the right brain hemisphere. This is due to the fact that impulses travel slightly faster along the auditory pathways leading to the opposite side of the head. Or, to put it more technically, contralateral inhibition of the nerve signal is less than ipsolateral inhibition.

Because, in the majority of people, the left side of the brain processes information logically and analytically, it is often better at testing the truth of hard evidence. Right-handers, of course, may only be able to do this easily provided they do not have to take written notes.

If the message you are attending to is better dealt with at an intuitive level, for example when trying to assess someone's emotional state, try placing the handset against your *left* ear. This means the sounds will reach the right side of the brain slightly faster than they arrive at the left.

Because the right hemisphere of most people's brains deals more with intuition and imagination, this may increase your sensitivity to unspoken messages.

DEALING WITH DIFFICULT CALLS

There are some telephone calls we all dread receiving— or having to make.

I shall be providing specific techniques for dealing with 11 of the toughest messages you ever have to get across in a moment.

But here are five general guidelines you can use with any type of disagreeable telephone call. While nothing can

turn it into a pleasant experience, these practical suggestions should make life a little easier.

1 Whenever possible take the initiative and make the
   call. That way you'll be able to prepare your message
   in advance instead of being caught unawares.
2 Get straight to the point. Never attempt to soften the
   blow by skirting around the problem. Say something
   like, 'My reason for calling is . . .' then launch into it.
3 If you are caught unawares, never respond immediately. Make an excuse and return the call when you
   have thought through your answers.
4 Use your knowledge of communication personalities
   described in Chapter Three (see pp. 62–4) when planning your response. Appeal to a Mastermind's desire
   for status, play on the emotions of Mothers, counter a
   Mechanic's arguments with hard facts, and take advantage of the Motivator's low threshold of boredom.
5 Check your understanding of the outcome. Before
   finishing the call, repeat back the actions you expect
   to be taken. This is important since, especially when
   even slightly tense, we tend to hear what we *expect* to
   hear rather than what has actually been said.
      Also repeat key points at suitable moments in the
   conversation. Far from being a waste of time such
   repetitions prevent much wasted effort.

How to Handle Calls You Hate to Make

Chasing Debts from a Key Customer

The secret of getting this message across is tactful firmness.
There's absolutely no point in beating about the bush or
pretending that you've phoned merely to inquire about his
or her health. Such messages not only ring false, but strike

the wrong note. The best course is to be businesslike and direct.

If you hate chasing people for money, it might be a good idea to write down the key points you want to get across. Certainly it's essential to be very clear about your facts, with invoice and order numbers, dates and so forth to hand.

If you know from experience that your customer is a past master of financial brinkmanship, employing any number of excuses to delay payment to the very last minute, then rehearse appropriate responses to his likely tactics so as not to be wrong-footed.

If, for instance, he uses the classic 'The cheque's in the post', claimed by many to be one of the world's three greatest lies, the best response is to acknowledge this whilst leaving yourself an opportunity to come back with a further chase when, as is likely, it fails to arrive. 'Can you tell me when it was posted so that we can look out for it?' is a good reply since it obliges him to be more specific.

If the answer you get is 'A couple of days ago', respond by suggesting that if it does not arrive by the following post you'll assume it's been mislaid and send a messenger round—if this is appropriate—to collect a fresh one.

Three keys to success:
- Plan these calls carefully, anticipating all the likely delaying tactics.
- Mentally rehearse the call.
- Stay polite but be direct.

Dealing with Valid Complaints

Stay calm and don't be provoked, however aggressive the caller. If you lose your temper you'll only escalate the anger to a point where no useful dialogue can take place.

What's more, you'll probably lose that customer even if his or her complaint is eventually satisfied.

Allow the caller to let off steam, while responding in a neutral way, by remarking, 'I see', 'I understand' and so on.

Never allow yourself to be browbeaten into apologising too soon. Extract all the information you can in order to build up as accurate a picture as possible of the nature, extent and validity of the complaint. Dig deeper by asking open-ended questions such as: 'Was any other difficulty encountered?' or 'Did the service fail to satisfy in any other way as well?'

If you don't have sufficient information immediately to hand to answer the complaint efficiently, then take the caller's number and say you will return her call as soon as you've checked out the situation.

Do not keep her hanging on the line while you look up files, consult colleagues or get information from the computer. Having to hold on only makes the caller even more exasperated.

Even if you could answer right away, it's sometimes a good strategy to offer to return her call, which not only allows her time to cool off but also gives you the upper hand since you've initiated the call. This places her psychologically in your debt as you've done something for her.

If you are in the wrong, then say so and apologise politely and fully—without abasing yourself or making your company seem too inefficient. Offer whatever is in your power to make amends. Give her your name and number and suggest that if she has any further difficulties she should call you directly.

Making yourself into her friend will not only take the sting out of the complaint but give your company a well-satisfied customer who is likely to place fresh orders in

227

the future. In fact, properly handled, a complaint can be transformed into a great selling opportunity.

Three keys to success:
- Be polite, but not abjectly apologetic.
- Find out all the facts before deciding on your best course of action.
- Call him or her back. It puts you in a position of strength.

Making Complaints

Before dialling, decide exactly what you want to get out of the call: your cash refunded, replacement of faulty goods, better service, an apology, or whatever.

Check your facts carefully. Have all the evidence necessary to support your case to hand before placing the call.

Always telephone rather than writing. People are much more likely to act on your complaint when spoken to directly, and far more information can be communicated in a brief call than by means of even a lengthy letter.

If you get fobbed off with excuses, use the 'cracked record' technique described on p. 231. This involves repeating your demands over and over again until you get satisfaction.

Avoid being personal or losing your temper. Be polite but firm.

Always talk to the most senior person possible. The higher you go the faster your complaint will be dealt with.

Three keys to success:
- Plan the call carefully. Check facts and know what you want to achieve.
- Be polite and never get personal.
- Speak to the most senior person possible.

Calling the Bank Manager to Extend your Credit

For this call to have any chance of succeeding, you have to have already done two things before picking up the receiver.

The first is to have established a friendly, one-to-one relationship with the manager. He or she must know you as a person rather than merely an account number. Secondly, you have to have kept the manager informed of your company's financial state and flagged any likely overshoot on the overdraft, perhaps caused by a particularly slow cash-flow towards the end of the month. There is nothing managers hate more than surprises and the more a request takes them by surprise, the less likely they are to respond favourably.

Keep the call brief and businesslike. Always support it by written information, clearly stating why the overdraft extension is required and when the situation can be expected to rectify itself. This can be either faxed or delivered by messenger. Both give an appropriate sense of efficiency. Never leave the call until the last minute or it will seem like a panic measure. Forward planning should warn of any likely shortfalls in the finances.

Three keys to success:
- Get straight to the point: never waste the manager's time or your own by beating about the bush.
- Have all the necessary facts and figures at your fingertips. Prepare and plan the call carefully.
- Support your request by written details which can be faxed.

229

Persuading a Superior He's Wrong without Ruining Your Promotion Prospects

How you plan this call depends on the personality of your boss, and what sort of a relationship you have with him or her. Some bosses actually favour a no-nonsense approach and will respect you for being a straight talker.

In these cases the call can be as direct as you wish. Stay calm but sound confident and assertive. This can only be achieved by preparing the ground carefully, being absolutely certain of your facts and ready to counter any objections she raises.

If the boss is likely to explode with rage at the merest suggestion she could be in the wrong, you'll have to adopt a more subtle and devious strategy. This consists of persuading her that she has actually dreamed up the plan you favour in the first place.

Exactly how this is achieved will depend on the extent of the difference between what you and she propose. If the ideas are close on several points, start by stressing these key similarities and praising her for coming up with such key ideas.

When you come to the point where you feel she has erred, try saying something like 'To be honest, I wasn't quite clear on this point. I assume that your game plan is to . . .' then describe your own proposals, 'since this will allow us to . . .' and add the benefit which this idea will provide, or the pitfall it will avoid.

Provided the boss has a glimmer of insight she will immediately see where her own plan was flawed and delightedly adopt your own proposals as her true intention. A really honest boss will even acknowledge that you are right and that her initial approach was in error.

230

Three keys to success:
- Work out exactly why and how your boss's plans go wrong.
- Be very certain of your facts before challenging the boss.
- With a boss who can't bear to be wrong, make him or her believe your ideas were really his or her own.

Sacking a Supplier with whom You've Developed a Close Relationship

Most people want to be liked, which is why we hate saying something hurtful or upsetting. But if the supplier, after fair warning, is still fouling things up, you could be faced with a choice of saying goodbye either to it or your own business.

As with every important call, preparation is essential. You may also find it less stressful to rehearse the call with a colleague.

Phone the colleague and role-play the situation anticipating the likely reaction of your supplier based on knowledge of his or her personality. Your colleague then tries out the most likely reactions, enabling you to polish your responses.

Do not beat about the bush but get right down to it. Say something along these lines: 'Normally I'd have written you a letter, but because of the close relationship we've built up over the last couple of years I thought it only reasonable to tell you this myself. We are going to have to dispense with your services for these reasons . . .' and then list them.

If you do not want to get involved in a lengthy discussion, use the cracked record technique, which involves simply repeating the basic facts over and over

231

again, without allowing yourself to get drawn into side issues.

Before placing the call be clear in your mind which of these three objectives you want to achieve.

1 Getting rid of him for good;
2 Giving him a final warning, while being prepared to allow one last chance;
3 Firing a warning shot across his bows in the hope of improving quality or delivery.

The worst trap you call fall into is to start out meaning to do (1) but end up achieving (3). He'll regard you as a pushover for ever more.

Three keys to success:
- Know what you want to achieve.
- Rehearse the call by role-playing with a colleague.
- Use the cracked record to avoid getting drawn into distracting side issues.

Asking for a Refund

Fear of rejection prevents many people standing up for their rights, and these include asking for a refund when entitled to one. Yet the telephone is an ideal medium for making such a request. It is personal enough to make a refusal far less likely than if you'd merely written a letter, yet at one remove from the person being called, which means less stress than during a face-to-face encounter.

Start by establishing that the person you are calling is in a position to offer the refund. There's no point in chatting to a receptionist, for instance, when only the sales manager has the authority to repay the money. So begin your call by discovering which person in the organisation handles that problem. If it's a large company the chances

232

are there will be somebody whose job description includes precisely this task.

When you are put through, start by asking the person's name. It allows you to develop a far more personal and friendly conversation.

Explain you have been put through because you wish to talk about a refund and confirm he or she is in a position to deal with the problem.

Calmly and clearly explain the reason for your call. Have the necessary facts and figures, such as date of purchase, order number and so forth close to hand. Your ability to respond promptly and accurately to such basic questions will greatly increase her respect for you.

If you want a refund make that point right from the start and don't allow yourself to be diverted into accepting lesser offers. If you are met with a refusal persist for a while, then ask to speak to her superiors. Confirm any agreement reached by letter or fax immediately after ending the call.

Three keys to success:
- Make sure you are speaking to somebody with authority to offer a refund.
- State your case clearly and accurately.
- Never lose your temper, even when faced by an initial refusal.

Cold Canvassing Business Leads

Most people dislike cold calling. But once you get used to rejections, it can prove an extremely effective way of generating new business.

The first step is to be put through to the person you need to talk to, which often means getting past a secretary or receptionist. She or he may demand to know the nature of your business. Here are two tried and trusted ways of getting past this barrier.

First: 'My name is . . . and I'm a partner (or whatever) with . . . I'm calling to talk about your company's next financial statement and it's very important I speak to . . . Will you please put me through?'

A shorter but usually effective technique is simply to say: 'I'm calling long distance, will you please put me through . . .'

Having got through, you have perhaps 15 seconds to capture your potential customer's interest, so it is crucial to use an attention-grabbing opening.

Tried and trusted methods include asking a provocative question: 'Would you like to make an extra £1000 a month?' or using a personal reference: 'I'm calling at the suggestion of Bill Jones, he felt you could benefit from our services . . .'

Alternatively you might try making an offer he simply cannot refuse: 'I'd like to tell you about a proven method for increasing your profits by up to 75 per cent. It's already being used by major multinational companies . . .'

Three keys to success:
- Avoid a time of day when the person called is likely to be especially busy.
- Be prepared for secretaries and receptionists attempting to block your call.
- Use an attention-grabbing opening statement. The longer you can talk the better your chances of closing a sale or winning an appointment.

Selling an Idea to a Colleague

As I have mentioned before, people only really pay attention to messages they believe offer something positive for themselves. To sell an idea, first see how it will look from your colleague's viewpoint. Next decide which approach is most likely to make your colleague see the personal benefits in your message, for example, making her look good with the boss by increasing efficiency, reducing the time spent on routine tasks, raising her level of sales and so on.

State these reasons clearly and with enthusiasm. You must sound convinced and convincing in order to be persuasive. Pick your moment for making the call with care; avoid times when you know she'll be extra busy.

Three keys to success:
- See your idea through his or her eyes.
- Present it so that he or she can immediately see the personal benefits in your proposal.
- Be enthusiastic. If you don't sound convinced you'll never persuade others.

Criticising an Enthusiastic but Careless Subordinate

Use the PIN approach which I discussed earlier to safeguard their enthusiasm while correcting any errors.

Start by noticing and praising all the *Positive* aspects of his or her performance. This will make him pay attention to what you are saying. If you start out with criticism he'll probably stop listening quite quickly.

Next seek out any *Interesting* aspects of his conduct. This helps him see how his performance might be improved. Putting these neutral comments after the praise brings him down from the clouds of your praise without losing attention.

Only when these two stages are gone through should you consider the *Negative* aspects of his performance. But always do this in a constructive way, explaining clearly

235

how and why the mistake arose and what can be done to avoid it on future occasions.

Place your call as soon after the action as possible, since the quicker achievements are praised and mistakes pointed out the more likely your call is to change behaviour.

Three keys to success;
- Make the call as soon as possible
- Start by commenting on positive features.
- When pointing out mistakes offer practical suggestions as to how performance can be improved. Be specific rather than general.

Receiving Unjustified Complaints

Never take any complaints against your company personally. If the caller is aggressive try to keep calm. Simply listen with occasional 'mmms' and 'ahs' until his or her anger has subsided. Attempting to reason with angry callers, or to stop them in mid-flow, is useless—even when they have their facts wrong.

Much of their anger will be defused if you listen sympathetically. Being a good listener often turns you from foe to friend.

As when dealing with objections at a face-to-face meeting (Chapters Eight and Thirteen), encourage the caller to state *all* her complaints before you start dealing with any of them. This prevents her finding something new to grumble about just when you felt the problem was resolved.

Never use terms like 'problem' or 'grievance' which reinforce her indignation. Instead use phrases like 'this situation' or 'that approach'.

Restate her complaint in your own words. This clarifies the key issues in your own mind whilst helping defuse the caller's emotional attachment to them.

Never be tempted to appease her anger by making

promises you cannot fulfil. If uncertain what to do for the best, say you'll phone back once you're fully in the picture. But if you do that be sure to return her call.

Three keys to success:
- Stay calm even when being shouted out.
- Listen carefully and sympathetically. It can turn you into a friend.
- Never make promises you cannot keep. It only makes the original mistake worse.

GETTING YOUR MESSAGE ACROSS TO AN ANSWERING MACHINE

Some people refuse to talk to a machine, others find themselves suddenly tongue-tied as it beeps into action. Perhaps that's how you feel. But never waste time by refusing to speak or leaving a message which does not get at least part of what you wanted to say across.

Here are some practical ways to make the most of answering machines.

- Ignore the fact you are talking onto tape. Imagine a human being at the other end.
- Date and time your message. That way it is far less likely to get overlooked.
- Speak more slowly than normal so your message can be clearly understood the first time the tape is played. It irritates people if they have to rewind the cassette to listen to a garbled message for a second or third time.
- Repeat names, addresses or phone numbers. They can be hard to catch the first time round.
- Keep your message brief.

237

TEN TIPS FOR GETTING YOUR MESSAGE ACROSS BY PHONE

1   With business calls, always begin by saying good morning, good afternoon or good evening. This is not only courteous but also allows the other person time to tune into your name and focus on the likely purpose of your call.

   If the other person has placed the call, his or her mind tends to wander while waiting for the receiver to be picked up, even when this is within three rings of 12 seconds (an established benchmark for answering a ringing phone in many organisations). As a result he often fails to pay attention to the first second or so of your reply. If you immediately answer with the number or company name, the caller may not be fully attentive and could get confused or ask you to repeat it. It wastes time—yours and theirs—and is easily avoided.

   After you have said good morning or good afternoon, then identify the company and/or number to reassure the caller he has dialled correctly or, if it is a wrong number, to establish this fact promptly in order not to waste time.

   Finally, give the person your name, which establishes a positive relationship right from the start. It makes your organisation, and you personally, sound welcoming and friendly.

   Never ask a stranger, 'How are you?' It sounds phoney. Never tell them, 'You don't know me.' It betrays a lack of confidence.

2   Time your business calls carefully. The worst times are usually first thing in the morning or last thing at night.

238

Always ask, 'Is this a good time to talk briefly, or should I call you back?' Offer a specific time for calling again should the person say they cannot talk at that moment: 'Would 10.15 be suitable?'

3   Ensure that your message is listened to by using AIDA. The initials stand for four key elements of all successful calls.

A   Attention. You must make the caller sit up and take notice of what you have to say, in order to avoid becoming the victim of distracted listening.

I   Interest. In order to sustain attention, your message must satisfy the WIIFM factor.

D   Desire. Your message should create a desire in the other person.

A   Action. Your message should end with some clearly defined course of action.

4   Always use the caller's name. When given a name for the first time impress it onto your memory through silent repetition and frequent use. Remember people are most interested in themselves! Researchers analysing 500 American phone calls found the word 'I' had been used more than 4,000 times!

When your call ends, note down the person's name together with any other personal information given during the conversation, such as the names and ages of his children. File this carefully. It will help you develop an even warmer relationship during later calls.

5   Smile while phoning. It not only makes you sound enthusiastic but boosts your energy levels. A smile releases chemicals in the brain which increase feelings of confidence and optimism.

6   Always make 'thank you' calls whenever you're pleased with somebody. They work wonders for future

co-operation. But never delay your thanks. The closer they are to the action which pleased you the more powerful their effect.

7   Try to get an insight into how your caller thinks. Although this is often tricky, here are some ways of reducing the guesswork.

- Don't try to make an objective analysis based on voice quality. There are too many unknown quantities for the logical left brain to work with. Rely instead on your intuitive right brain. As you listen, stay relaxed and allow ideas about the speaker to drift into your mind. Such unforced impressions can often prove remarkably accurate.
- A rapid rate of speaking (provided the content also makes good sense) reveals above average intelligence.
- Hesitations, stammering, pauses often betray areas of anxiety or indecision.
- Depending on the context, emphasis placed on certain phrases may reveal a subconscious like or dislike of those ideas.
- From their conversation and approach try to discover whether you are talking to a Mastermind, Mother, Mechanic or Motivator.

  With a Mastermind explain how your proposals could enhance her success or enable goals to be achieved more easily. Persuade a Mother by describing the value of your message in terms of how people will benefit. With a Mechanic use facts and figures, while a Motivator's message needs to be as varied as possible.

8   Encourage co-operation by using the phrase 'Will that be all right?' this enables you to:

- Invite the other person to respond positively to your message;
- Bring him back into the conversation at any point where *you* need feedback about how your ideas are being received or emphasise a key part of your message;
- Subtly encourage him to agree with your message by replying that it 'will be all right'. This response is the most likely one, as people almost always do what is easiest. It takes a very stubborn person to respond negatively to such a cordial inquiry. And the more 'yeses' you get in response to your message the greater your chances of having the proposals accepted;
- Gain agreement at a later stage in the call. If you have used it a couple of times already, the phrase significantly increases your chances that a more demanding request will also prove acceptable.

    In some cases people like this phrase so much that they even copy the cadence and voice of the person using it.

9 Never answer the telephone when you are eating or drinking or while in the middle of a conversation with someone in the office. Never put one hand over the phone to speak to someone nearby; it makes you sound highly unprofessional.

10 Saying goodbye: the ability to end a telephone call efficiently is just as important as knowing how to get your message across in the first instance. Talk too long and you risk confusing, boring or irritating the other person.

    For a satisfactory conclusion to your message use the P–F–G strategy.

Be Polite. When dealing with a stranger, use his or her name in your final sentence. If there are some facts you particularly want remembered repeat them immediately before saying goodbye.

Be Firm. Avoid being diverted into an irrelevant discussion. If you find this hard to do, have a few plausible excuses such as 'Sorry, I'm wanted on the other phone' as a standby tactic. Usually, however, if your tone is positive, the other person will get the message. Having said farewell . . .

Be Gone. But always allow the caller to hang up first. If you put down the phone first it ends the call on a psychologically less than friendly note.

CHAPTER 15

Getting Your Message Across to the Media

Journalism, a profession whose business it is to explain to others what it personally does not understand.
Lord Northcliffe, English press mogul

The pollution leak had been a bad one. A junior employee at the giant agrochemical plant had turned the wrong valve, and thousands of tons of toxic waste gushed forth into a nearby river.

The inevitable result was poisoned waters, 20,000 dead fish, an outraged community and a story-hungry press. But when broadcast and print media journalists arrived at the plant in search of an explanation, all they found was a wall of silence.

The high steel gates were locked shut and nobody from the management was available for comment. In fact the only employee prepared to speak to the press was a big-bellied security man guarding the gate.

'I've been told to tell you guys no comment,' he explained in a firm but affable way. Then, seeing the massed media were totally unprepared to accept this response, he added casually and on the record: 'Anyhow, why is this such a great story? We only killed 20,000 fish for God's sake. Last month in Florida our sister company polluted a lake and killed half a million of them, yet not a word of that ever appeared in the press!'

My reporter friend who recounted this tale added that, immediately after the public relations fiasco, the company not only tightened up their procedures but also hired a press officer and sent their senior executives on a media training course.

These days, with ever-increasing press and public interest in the way all kinds of companies from multi-national giants to small local concerns conduct their business, it pays everyone likely to be thrust into the public eye to know how to get their message across to the media.

An invitation to talk to the press provides both an opportunity and a potential risk. An opportunity in that it allows you to publicise yourself, your organisation, your product or your service; to educate members of the public; to put your side of a controversial issue and to respond to comments or criticisms from others. It's a problem in that, if you come across badly or end up being misquoted, or quoted out of context, a bad situation can be made a great deal worse.

While there is no sure fire way of dealing with the media, the following guidelines should be helpful any time you find yourself thrust, willingly or extremely reluctantly, into the publicity spotlight.

Let's start by looking at some general points to bear in

mind whether you are talking to a newspaper or magazine journalist, speaking on radio or before television cameras.

TWELVE GUIDELINES FOR DEALING WITH THE MEDIA

1 Have a clear idea of what you want to say. Organise your thoughts. Write down and take to your interview a short list of the key points you want to make.

  Be prepared for obvious questions: 'What exactly is it your organisation does?' and aggressive ones: 'Why did you continue to market that product after research had so clearly shown it was damaging to health?'

  Keep your answer simple and direct in both cases. When the interview is hostile it is essential to keep your temper and answer as honestly and directly as possible. If you can avoid sounding shifty or evasive, the listeners and viewers are more likely to take your side against an obviously aggressive interviewer. Everybody roots for the underdog!

2 Keep responses concise and targeted. With radio and TV, paint with broad strokes and avoid nitty-gritty details which will not come across. Avoid quoting too many figures; at best it turns off your listeners entirely and at worst it confuses them. When forced to use figures, keep them simple and rounded. For example, instead of saying '57 per cent of our customers', say 'more than half of our customers'.

  For most TV and many radio programmes you are likely to have between three and five minutes to get your message across.

  Try to come up with at least one striking image or phrase which conveys the essence of your message.

245

Such comments, known in radio and TV as 'sound bites', should not last more than 20–30 seconds.

3   Arrange interviews on a face-to-face basis rather than over the telephone whenever possible as they reduce the risk of misunderstandings. Be clear what you will be discussing. Put yourself in the journalist's place and think about the sort of questions you would want to ask. When the interview is important have a colleague or relative role-play the reporter and ask you questions ranging from the polite and easily answered to the hard-hitting and hostile.

4   Brief yourself by reviewing all correspondence relating to the interview and get a verbal summary of all discussions leading up to the interview.

Try to find out what the interviewer or his/her publication has written/published/broadcast on that subject before. At the very least study a recent issue of the publication or view/listen to the programme concerned.

5   Never say 'No Comment', which comes across as if you have something to hide. Instead turn the question around, as described in (7) below, to come up with an answer you can give on the record.

6   Never regard probing questions as evidence of antagonism. In most instances this is merely good journalism. Keep calm, listen carefully and pause before responding—even when the answer springs to mind. As I explained earlier, this makes your reply seem more considered and thoughtful and, therefore, more persuasive.

7   Do not feel obliged to answer a question just because it has been asked. If the questions do not relate to the information you want to get across, bridge the gap by introducing the points you are concerned to raise. You might do this by saying, 'You've raised an interesting

issue, but I think that rather more relevant to the current situation is . . .'

8   Plan your time so as not to shorten the interview. Often the most important part comes towards the end.

9   Discover in advance whether additional background material or visual aids could be helpful in putting your point of view across and have those ready. Decide too whether you will need technical back-up from your company's specialists. If so, make certain the relevant staff are fully briefed and prepared.

10 If publicity would be helpful to your company, court it by developing good contacts among local and/or national media journalists and feature writers.

11 Use the same body language on radio and television as you would during a face-to-face meeting. If your usual conversational style involves lots of gestures and facial expression that's how you should talk when speaking into a microphone (but see TV exception below). By mirroring your emotions in your face and body you will improve the pace and flow of your speech, and make your voice sound far more relaxed, confident and natural.

12 Provided your message is upbeat and positive, smile even if being interviewed on radio. This makes you sound warmer, friendlier and more enthusiastic. Remember that by listening to you, your listeners are inviting you into their home, office or car. If you sound friendly they will be glad to have done so.

Courting Publicity

When a story on which you have special knowledge or expertise is in the news, call your contacts and offer to provide a comment. Usually they will be only too delighted to include such authoritative comments in the story and this can provide you with valuable personal and/or corporate publicity.

The media are constantly seeking expert commentary on news events in the area of corporate and financial news. But be careful. By placing yourself in the public eye and courting useful publicity, you will also be setting yourself up as a target for negative as well as positive stories.

The Do's and Don'ts of Appearing on TV

Do avoid striped shirts or ties which tend to create a disagreeable pattern on the screen. You may even be asked to change if your shirt or tie is unsuitable.

White shirts and blouses do not generally come across well, especially on video, because of the greater contrast range. A light blue is usually better but may prove unacceptable if the studio intends using what is called a 'blue screen' to add background or special effects.

This is how, for example, weather bulletins are broadcast. The weather man or woman stands in front of a perfectly blank, blue-painted screen on which the weather maps are added using computer technology. Although unable to see anything on the screen behind him, he can keep track of where to point by glancing at a monitor to one side of the camera, which shows the same image as viewers are seeing at home.

For your interview the director may want to place you against, for example, a city background. She will do this using the same type of technology used for the weather maps. This means that if you went on wearing a blue shirt or blouse parts of the background would appear across your chest!

Always check with the researcher or producer what colours will be best.

Do avoid bright and distracting designs on your clothes.

You want people to pay attention to what you have to say—not to your dress sense.

Don't always expect make-up facilities, especially at small regional stations. Even when the interviewer is made up you may not be offered that option. Be prepared by taking along your own flesh-coloured powder, such as Max Factor, to cover blemishes and prevent your skin looking shiny under the bright studio lights.

If being made up by a professional, ask her or him to give you some 'eye definition' to stop your eyes from seeming to sink into your face. This is especially important if you have very light eye colouring.

Use a tanning lotion the night before you are due to broadcast to give yourself a safe, but natural-looking tan. This reduces the amount of make-up needed and makes you look fitter and healthier.

Don't be tempted to dart glances at the camera. It makes you look shifty. Keep your eyes on the interviewer. Try not to blink too much either since this is distracting to the audience.

If you want to emphasise a particular point by speaking directly to the audience, then face the 'live' camera, which can be easily identified by the red light glowing on the top. But beware! Speaking directly to camera requires experience if it is to come across in a relaxed and effective manner.

Do be ready to talk to a camera rather than a flesh and blood interviewer. If you are invited for a brief interview by a local television station, you could well find the person asking you questions is miles away in another studio, with his voice reaching you via a small earpiece. You will be left facing either a camera and operator, or sometimes even just a remotely controlled camera in an otherwise empty studio.

In this case be sure to deliver your answers directly into

the camera lens. As far as the viewers are concerned you will seem to be talking to the interviewer. Even if there is a monitor to one side or above the camera, refrain from glancing at it to see how you look. The effect will be to make you look shifty and devious by refusing to give 'eye contact'—so far as the viewer is concerned—to the person conducting your interview.

It may help if you mentally superimpose the face of somebody you know and like over the black eye of the lens. You'll find it easier to talk in a relaxed and conversational way to another person, even if he or she is there only in your imagination.

Do watch body language when being interviewed under the circumstances described above. In a full studio, with several camera angles to choose from, the director can cut between shots, but with just one camera you will be framed to show your head and shoulders only. If you use too many gestures, to the viewer your hands will be only little pink objects bobbing distractingly in and out of shot. In this situation restrain your use of gesture.

Do pay attention to small details of your appearance. A loose button, a trail of thread, specks of dandruff on your shoulders will all become glaringly obvious in close-up. Check how you look in a mirror before going on camera, or get an observant colleague to give you a critical once-over.

Don't slouch; it will look terrible on screen. Keep your posture straight but relaxed. Imagine you are talking to just one person rather than an audience which may number millions. Remember that to a viewer you are speaking directly and solely to him.

Do send out appropriate body-language signals when listening to the questions. Do not lean away or fold your arms. Nod occasionally to show the viewer non-verbally that you are paying close attention.

Do keep constantly in mind that television is about

impressions rather than facts. After the interview is over what is most likely to stay in the audience's mind is not *what* you said so much as *how* you said it. Your goal is to come across as positive, confident, calm and friendly.

Don't go on too long. Try to provide a well-focused answer in 45 seconds or less. You can only do this by stating the key point clearly in the second or third sentence of your answer, before following up with equally clear supporting arguments.

The Do's and Don'ts of Appearing on Radio

In many ways this is a more relaxed medium than television, even when the show is going out live. There is less technology to worry about, and your appearance counts for nothing over the airwaves so you don't have to dress up for it.

Even so a few do's and don'ts will help you get the best out of radio interviews.

Do smile a lot to warm up your voice and make you sound confident.

Don't be afraid to use gestures which can add rhythm and pace to your words. I have seen DJs on all-night shows waving their arms around like manic windmills, all by themselves in the wee small hours of the morning. They know it makes their delivery seem more energetic, enthusiastic and natural.

Do prepare for the interview by checking facts and figures. If you are asked a question to which you don't know the answer, then say so. Risk winging it and you may be caught out on air. It's just not worth the risk.

Don't be afraid of the microphone. Microphone fright, described in Chapter Fourteen, can strike even normally articulate people dumb. Speak directly to the interviewer instead and ignore the microphone. Engage in a conversation with her or him exactly as if you were chatting in your own front room.

If, as occasionally happens, you are talking from a remote studio with just the microphone for company and the interviewer's voice reaching you via headphones, imagine yourself sitting opposite your best friend and talk to them in the same comfortable manner.

Do keep answers simple and avoid too much detail. Unlike TV, where statistical information could be supported on screen by charts and so forth, all your radio listeners have to go on is what you tell them. If the message starts getting too complicated they will simply turn off mentally or, physically, by retuning to a friendly station.

CHAPTER 16

Getting Your Message Across with Overseas Audiences

If you wish to be thoroughly misinformed about a country, consult a man who has lived there for thirty years and speaks the language like a native.
George Bernard Shaw quoting Lord Palmerston

A friend of mine, an accomplished speaker on the international lecture circuit, recently found himself in something of a quandary. He was due to address a large meeting of Japanese and North American executives in a Tokyo hotel. His dilemma was this. North American audiences expect the speaker to relax them by starting out with a joke. For Japanese audiences such an approach is anathema. They expect speakers to be serious and, if they really want to gain their respect, humble. Far from making a bad impression, apology for personal inadequacy as a speaker is seen as a sign of laudable modesty and great sincerity, two essential qualities when addressing a Pacific Rim audience.

What was my friend to do with this mixed group? Tell a joke and offend his Japanese listeners, or humble himself and make the Americans think he lacked confidence as a lecturer?

His compromise was, I think, an extremely neat one. Rising to his feet, he confessed his dilemma: 'If you were all Americans, I would start with a joke. If you were all Japanese, I would begin by apologising. So let me apologise to you for not telling a joke!'

This anecdote illustrates an essential point to be grasped by anyone who has to get their message across to an overseas audience. Crossing the cultural divide is not simply a matter of speaking more slowly, but of considering your whole style of presenting, both verbal and non-verbal, together with the structure and content of your message.

If you are given the task of speaking to an audience from a different culture, be sure to do your homework. Read books on that culture; speak to colleagues who have already spoken in that culture and, despite George Bernard Shaw's scornful dismissal of expatriates, talk to long-time residents in that country whenever possible.

Learn what works and what may cause unintentional offence. Know which approach will ease your message across cultural barriers and which is likely to kill it dead.

There are, to take just one instance, significant differences in the amount and type of information your message should contain for different audiences. In Sweden, for example, audiences try to define the strategic implications of a message by asking more theoretical questions. North American audiences, by contrast, prefer to explore the way things are going to work in the real world by means of practical questions.

You should also bear in mind four key cultural differences:

- The use of time
- Individualism vs collectivism
- The role of orderliness and conformity
- Patterns of communication.

The information given below is derived from several sources: my own experience of lecturing in many countries around the world, information supplied to me by business people attending my presentation training seminars and a wide range of articles and books.

It is never easy to sum up the complex elements of any culture and to provide a thumbnail sketch of what makes a country or a people tick without appearing simplistic and patronising. I have done my best to list the pitfalls and attitudes in major countries and regions of the world in a way that will prove of practical value to those faced with the challenge of getting their messages cross away from home base.

But it is important to bear in mind two points. First, the younger generations in most nations of the world are, in many ways, more like one another than they are like their own previous generations. Because of its pervasive influence many of the attitudes and attributes of North American culture have now been exported to the youth of the world. For this reason you may find that younger executives behave more like a US audience than the comments below might suggest.

The second point is that nothing teaches you about communicating across cultures and in different countries better than personal experience. So use the notes below as a first step rather than the last word when speaking overseas.

Before dealing with specific countries, let's take an overview of that fastest-growing of all world markets, the Pacific Rim.

CULTURAL FACTORS IN THE PACIFIC RIM

These so-called Tiger economies have a shared history characterised by sophisticated cultural achievements, dynastic rule and social stratification.

Use of Time

You will require great patience since every stage of a negotiation is slower in this part of the world than in North America and Europe.[1] There are three reasons for this:

1   Far greater emphasis is placed on establishing long-term relationships than on negotiating quick deals. They want to get to know you as a person, before fully trusting your message.
2   Typically there are several people on each negotiating team and consensus is vitally important.
3   Decisions are usually made by the whole group at almost every level. The good news is that, once made, such decisions are usually rapidly implemented.

Individualism vs Collectivism

The Pacific Rim has a 'we' rather than, as in North America and Europe, a 'me' culture.

It is important to help your counterpart 'save face' and to accept a need for agreement on all points.

---

1 Negotiations in Singapore and Hong Kong typically move more rapidly than in other parts of the Pacific Rim.

The Role of Orderliness and Conformity

A strong need for orderliness and conformity helps explain the importance of building a close relationship with your counterparts. This is seen as a way of bringing order and certainty to the discussion.

Centuries of the Confucian ethic make social relationships extremely important. They are the basis for such traditions as courtesy, formality in behaviour, excessive politeness, group loyalty and identification, avoidance of conflicts, and extreme modesty when talking about one's status, accomplishments and family.

Patterns of Communication—Verbal

The influence of Confucianism, Buddhism and Taoism in Pacific Rim cultures has placed a premium on such aspects of communication as humility, silence, modesty and mistrust of words.

Because of this, messages are generally conveyed subtly and indirectly. Speakers expect audiences to *know* what is in their minds rather than spelling it out directly as one would for Europeans or North Americans. As a result you may find yourself being given all the information necessary with the exception of the most crucial piece! This you are supposed to work out for yourself by listening between the lines.

Rather than a direct 'no', for example, refusals will be conveyed via comments such as 'We will study the matter' or 'We want to get more opinions on your idea.' This makes it essential to use positive listening in order to pick up on the subtext to their messages.

Patterns of Communication—Non-Verbal

As a general rule body language is far more reserved than in the West. You seldom observe expressive gestures and eye contact is usually fleeting.

Although personal space is somewhat smaller than in North America and Europe, touching between colleagues is generally restrained. Brief handshakes or bows are more typical than hugs and other forms of greeting.

To Survive in Social Settings

Do learn to use chopsticks. If you want to serve food to another diner and there are no serving tools, reverse your chopsticks then pick up the food with the unused ends.

When eating rice, the Chinese and Japanese will raise the bowl and scoop it into their mouths. Koreans leave the bowl on the table and lift the food to the mouth with chopsticks or a spoon. They look on raising the rice bowl to the lips as ill-bred in the extreme.

If you drop your chopsticks do not worry. Your host will look on this as a lucky omen. It means you will be invited back for another meal.

Don't be offended if Asians slurp their soup noisily and suck in noodles. It is the normal way to eat.

Don't leave your chopsticks stuck vertically into the food bowl so they resemble incense sticks. A widespread Asian superstition says this is unlucky since it means the meal is meant for the dead and not the living.

Don't accept an invitation unless it has been extended at least three times.

Do wait for your host to seat you. Seating arrangements are usually complex and vary according to the size and shape of the table, the kind of room you will be eating in and the occasion itself.

Do pay the bill after a casual meal when you are selling something. If eating with friends, the person who wants to pay will go quietly to the cashier before the meal ends and pay.

Don't separate business and social life. Most Asian companies want long-term business relationships and will be sizing you up as people they would like to play with as well as work with.

Asians love drinking and can usually hold their liquor. If you do not drink, say so. They will not be offended.

Do join in the Karaoke (it means empty bathtub in Japanese and refers to the human enjoyment of singing in the bath).

Getting Your Message Across to Japanese Audiences

The Japanese strive for perfection in all they do. They possess a strong sense of purpose and the ability to sacrifice individual interests to the common good, combined with immense industry.

Japanese society is extremely status-conscious so always wear the right clothes. This usually means sporting designer-label products which are supreme status symbols. Avoid casual dress. The Japanese male business dress code *always* demands a conservative suit and tie.

Incorrect attention to status is one of the most common mistakes made by Westerners in their dealings with the Japanese. In Japan executives expect to be treated with the respect demanded by their status within the company and will afford Westerners the same consideration. Make certain, therefore, that your business cards give you the highest status your company or organisation is prepared to bestow and carry these with you at all times. You never know when you'll be called on to provide one.

A few years ago, while lecturing in Hong Kong, I spent a pleasant afternoon swimming in the rooftop pool of the Grand Hyatt Hotel overlooking the harbour. Swimming beside me was a Japanese businessman and we started talking. After several lengths of the pool he inquired politely: 'You have business card?'

'Not on me,' I admitted, glancing down at my swimming costume. He smiled and, from his own skimpy trunks, produced a laminated business card.

Japanese audiences look for sincerity, plus a somewhat indirect message, full of ambiguities and inner meanings. Avoid giving an impression of exaggeration and always provide detailed background information for any of your proposals.

Their emphasis on collectivism means that you should address your audience as a whole. Take care never to focus on or identify any specific group which will lead to other participants feeling ignored.

Getting Your Message Across to Chinese Audiences

Persistence and patience are essential virtues. Conducting business with the Chinese is like watching paint dry—only slower.

Time is not money to the Chinese. Time is time and money is money.

Beware middle management. They are often old Maoists whose chief function seems to be to prevent anything from ever getting done. Get your message across to the men—and sometimes women—at the top as quickly and directly as you can.

Beware of getting embroiled in factional disputes. The Chinese tend to place greater faith in the expertise of Western business people than in their own specialists; this can easily cause ill-feeling unless you are extremely tactful.

If an opportunity occurs to enhance your Chinese associate's status or position, use it. He is likely to reciprocate by moving your business forward.

GETTING YOUR MESSAGE ACROSS TO NORTH AMERICAN AUDIENCES

It is risky to lay down rules about the behaviour of North American audiences since the backgrounds and expectations of audiences vary so widely from coast to coast. A message which goes across perfectly in Manhattan, for example, may flop in Jackson, Mississippi, or Calgary, Alberta, or Montreal, Quebec. Nonetheless, here are some general hints as to what they, and you, can expect.

Use of Time

The pace is vigorous in North America, especially in the United States. The emphasis is on getting your message across as quickly and efficiently as possible.

Do not be surprised, however, if final buying decisions are sometimes slowed down by financial, strategic planning, legal or other managers. This slow and exhaustive review is sometimes known as the 'paralysis of analysis'.

Individualism vs Collectivism

Individualism is prized in North America, with social status based on financial success.

Though family commitments and outside interests are extremely common and deeply held, an emphasis on business and financial success is usual, especially in the United States.

261

The Role of Orderliness and Conformity

The need for both is low compared with other parts of the world. This is a nation of individuals who like to flaunt their unique, personal identity: a 'me' far more than a 'we' culture.

How business is done is considered less important than getting it done efficiently.

While North Americans are generally informal in their business presentations, French-speaking Canada has greater formality than is found elsewhere in North America.

Patterns of Communication—Verbal

Verbal communications are direct and open. Silence is to be avoided and interruptions are common.

Patterns of Communication—Non-Verbal

North Americans like a personal space of around three feet in business situations. Little touching occurs. Handshakes are firm but brief. You rarely see two North American business people hugging each other upon meeting or parting. Once again French-speaking Canada is an exception to this general rule.

Some North American executives are 'back slappers' but even this gesture tends to be brief and often not appreciated by others. A peck on the cheek or a hug may be used between women or between a man and a woman who have known one another for a while.

Eye contact lasts for between five and seven seconds, with breaks of two or three seconds between each gaze. This is seen as showing interest, sincerity and truthfulness.

Be polite, direct and candid in your comments. US audiences want to hear it like it is. Indirect replies may be seen as betraying insincerity, a lack of confidence, or even dishonesty.

GETTING YOUR MESSAGE ACROSS TO MIDDLE EAST AUDIENCES

This widely diverse area of the world includes countries such as Saudi Arabia, Egypt, Jordan, Syria, Iran, Lebanon, Oman, the United Arab Emirates (UAE), and Israel. Arabs are small in number and centred mainly in Saudi Arabia, Jordan, Iraq and the Gulf States (The UAE[1] and Oman).

Such diversity means it is impossible to be specific about negotiating and communicating in this region, except for a few general observations. Note that the comments below apply in varying degrees to all countries in this area with the exception of Israel.

Bargaining is an essential part of everyday life in the Middle East, especially for Arabs. So be prepared to negotiate over even the most trivial of deals.

Religion plays a major role in both the history and present-day business environment of the Middle East. Through much of the area, there is no separation between religious and state authority.

Use of Time

'Time' is less precise than in Europe and North America and appointments are held in less esteem than in North America. Hurrying a Middle Easterner through a discussion could well be interpreted as an insult. It is also considered unlucky to plan too far ahead.

Middle Easterners refuse to let their lives be dominated by the clock. 'Two o'clock on Tuesday' probably means

1 UAE, founded in 1971, comprises Abu Dhabi, Dubai, Sharja, Ras al Khaimah, Ajman, Fujaira and Umm al Qaiwain.

any time on Tuesday afternoon. Do not take offence at any lack of punctuality: it is not intended as an insult nor does it denote any lack of interest in your message. It's just part of the culture and reflects the region's more recent agricultural background. When, for thousands of years, you've followed only the seasons, why start making exceptions for diary schedules?

Individualism vs Collectivism

Middle Eastern culture is strongly 'we' orientated. This is especially true when dealing with governments or quasi-governmental Arab organizations, such as oil companies.

Patterns of Communication—Verbal

The Arabs are a poetic people who admire eloquence and vivid story-telling. Try to paint word pictures and make your message as lyrical as possible.

Patterns of Communication—Non-Verbal

They say that if you were to cut off an Arab's arms you would make him dumb. Certainly the amount of gesturing, pointing and arm-waving which accompanies the average negotiation in the Middle East would seem to support this idea, so be as extravagant as you wish with your gestures.

The personal space in Middle Eastern countries tends to be a lot less than in Europe and North America. Some Western males feel uncomfortable when an Arab man stands so close to them. Learn to accept this apparent invasion of your personal space as an aspect of the culture into which nothing further need be read.

Gender Issues

The acceptance of women in business varies from one country to the next, with some being far more conservative than others. Men dominate UAE business society with local women being almost non-existent. Expatriate women, however, can be found in some professional and managerial positions. Arab women will rarely be found during business meetings, even when these take place in private homes.

Dress code is very important in many of the countries in this region, with women being expected to wear a long skirt and a loose-fitting, long-sleeved blouse.

GETTING YOUR MESSAGE ACROSS IN EASTERN EUROPE

Use of Time

Eastern Europeans are generally punctual, with scheduled meetings seldom starting more than 10 to 15 minutes after the appointed time.

Individualism vs Collectivism

The strong influence of Communism over several decades has created a 'we' consciousness which still predominates despite the break-up of the former Soviet Bloc. Consensus and the ideals of the group prevail in many discussions. This helps explain the lack of independence displayed by Eastern Europeans over business deals. Rather than take decisions themselves, they often insist on checking with superiors first, even on minor matters.

Be prepared too, for getting your message across to groups rather than individuals. Most negotiations and dis-

265

cussions involve a team which can result in a lack of focus and slowed decision making.

The Role of Orderliness and Conformity

The lumbering remains of cumbersome Communist bureaucracies result in duplication of effort and blurred lines of authority. Decisions tend to be handed down from the top, although it is often difficult to work out exactly who is in charge.

Patterns of Communication—Verbal

Communications are generally direct with straightforward requests and clear demands. Language barriers aside, guesswork is seldom necessary to establish their point of view.

Although they are gracious hosts, their manner of speaking can cause offence by seeming abrupt and aggressive. Do not construe such a response to you or your message as betraying either hostility or lack of enthusiasm.

Patterns of Communication—Non-Verbal

Personal space is usually less than in North America. On meeting and parting, shake hands firmly but briefly. An exception is handshaking between the sexes. These can be fairly lengthy in some East European countries, such as the Czech Republic and Poland, with the man kissing the woman's hand.

Hand and arm gestures are usually expressive, so do not be afraid to gesticulate when getting your message across.

266

GETTING YOUR MESSAGE ACROSS IN FRANCE

Use of Time

French business people are generally punctual and expect you to be on time as well.

Individualism vs Collectivism

To the despair of many French governments, the French people are very individualistic and like to go their own way, even at the expense of preventing mutually beneficial group consensus. At the same time most are intensely nationalistic and take great pride in every aspect of French culture which most regard as superior to all others in Europe.

The Role of Orderliness and Conformity

The French are somewhat formal and rather conservative in their business dealings, so make certain your message is well-researched and strong on concepts.

They use reason and logic rather than emotions when evaluating messages, which should be conveyed in an informative and even slightly subdued manner. North American-style hype and enthusiasm are likely to be poorly received, especially among older and more socially conservative French business people.

Patterns of Communication—Verbal

First-name use is initiated by the person who is older and superior in rank. Otherwise they are used only among close friends.

Patterns of Communication—Non-Verbal

Shake hands with a single, quick shake and light pressure upon meeting. On leaving, shake hands again with all those to whom you have been introduced.

GETTING YOUR MESSAGE ACROSS IN GERMANY

Use of Time

Punctuality is insisted upon and arriving late for a meeting, even with a good reason, could put you at a disadvantage.

Arrange appointments well in advance and at the highest possible level. Prepare an agenda for the meeting. Germans pay great attention to order and planning.

Individualism vs Collectivism

Until recently they operated a strong 'we' culture with individualism generally frowned upon by a highly conservative society. Although the consensus is now starting to crack somewhat as a result of economic pressures, they remain suspicious of people who appear significantly different from themselves.

The Role of Orderliness and Conformity

Germans often come across as formal and reserved at first meetings, and may strike those unfamiliar with the culture as unfriendly. They are not, but it does take time for them to feel comfortable with first names. Do not attempt to develop personal relationships beyond what is required for politeness. They prefer remaining aloof until the business has been completed. Younger Germans tend to be rather less formal.

When preparing your message pay attention to order and planning. Avoid ambiguity and communicate your message clearly and directly. Your tone and structure should be serious and formal. Make certain you are well prepared. Any proposals should be realistic, concrete and delivered in a clear, orderly and authoritative manner. Your supporting information must be detailed and logical and contain all the appropriate technical data.

If you are not certain of your facts it is better to say nothing than to venture what may be regarded as an ill-informed opinion.

Patterns of Communication—Verbal

Avoid first names unless you are specifically invited to use them. Anyone with a doctorate (such as a lawyer) must be addressed as Herr/Frau/Fräulein/Doktor...—, while a professor is referred to as Herr/Frau/Fräulein/Professor...—. Knowing and using titles is important and forgetting to do so would be considered impolite.

The Germans have a strong sense of privacy. Avoid asking personal questions apart from polite inquiries about their family.

Avoid telling jokes to break the ice as this could give the impression you are not sufficiently serious about the proposals.

Patterns of Communication—Non-Verbal

Always shake hands firmly on meeting and again on parting. It is impolite to have hands in your pockets while talking with a German.

You should dress neatly and conservatively in business settings where a suit, and for men a tie, are essential. Be polite and formal in your dealings. Do not try to establish personal relationships beyond normal courtesies.

Try speaking to smaller rather than larger groups if possible since the atmosphere in such meetings tends to be somewhat less stuffy.

GETTING YOUR MESSAGE ACROSS IN SPAIN

Use of Time

Always arrive punctually for meetings, even though this means you may be kept waiting. Business meetings generally start 15 or so minutes after the time agreed. Expect a relaxed pace of negotiations.

The Role of Orderliness and Conformity

Establish a solid relationship. Trust, rapport and compatibility are essential in order to do business in Spain.

Avoid putting your counterpart in an embarrassing position since pride and honour are extremely important to the Spanish.

Make your messages detailed and practical. Grandiose schemes are not well received.

Patterns of Communication—Verbal

Spanish surnames have two components: the father's family name followed by the mother's. Both are usually used in written messages (e.g. Sr Francisco Martínez Rodríguez). Married women retain their paternal surname with 'de' followed by their husband's (e.g. Sra Ana Pacheco de Martínez), although this tradition is not universally adhered to. In speech only one name is normally used (Señorita Martínez, Señora Pacheco *or* Martínez). Don and Doña are used with the first name to show respect (Don Francisco, Doña Ana.

Although a senior person may use your first name, only follow suit if you have been invited to do so.

Patterns of Communication—Non-Verbal

Shake hands on meeting and leaving. Men should wait for women to extend their hands first.

Abrazos, or hugs, are reserved for friends. Dress formally and speak with as much eloquence as you are able.

CHAPTER 17

Your Check Lists for Success

All the world's a stage,
And all the men and women merely players.
William Shakespeare, As You Like It

This final chapter contains a series of quick-reference check lists summarising the key points described elsewhere in this book. Use it as a rapid guide to ways of overcoming any barriers which may be arising as you seek to get your message across.

STRUCTURING YOUR MESSAGE

- Clarify ideas in your own mind before trying to communicate them to your audience.
- Express your thoughts in an organised manner.
- Keep the message tightly focused and avoid rambling.

- Avoid abstractions without giving concrete examples.
- Explain the meaning of complicated words and expressions.
- Avoid unfamiliar technical jargon and always explain terms when they are used.
- Never talk without sufficient preparation or knowledge.
- Never talk down to your audience.
- Summarise and conclude your message clearly.
- Never give people only facts. Illustrate with examples.
- Communicate in the same language as your audience. Familiar language builds rapport and trust.
- Remember the WIIFM factor. We all listen to the same radio station!
- Involve your audience. Use phrases such as 'Imagine you were involved', 'What would you do if . . .', 'Assuming you are in that position', 'Imagine you have just . . .'
- Establish your credibility early on or no one will listen.
- If your message contains a promise, be sure you follow through.

PRESENTING YOUR MESSAGE

- Avoid speaking too rapidly. Fast speech encourages shallow breathing and makes you more anxious.
- Avoid too high a vocal pitch. The lower the pitch the more authoritative you will sound.
- Avoid talking too softly. When speaking in an unfamiliar room check that you can be heard at the back before the meeting starts.
- Breathe using the abdomen to draw air deep into your lungs.
- Vary your voice. Change your speed, pitch and volume. Avoid speaking in a monotone.

273

- Slow down and drop your voice to signal that you are about to make a point of great interest and importance.
- Sound excited and enthusiastic. To persuade you must come across as persuaded.
- Never read your message unless there is no other option. Your attention should be focused on the audience not words on paper.
- If you do have to read the message, have it printed in large, triple-spaced type.
- Do not turn pages of notes over. Slide each to one side—gently.
- Never use more than 6–7 cue cards.
- Use key words only. Hand print or type these so they can be read at a glance.
- Write your opening and closing comments on separate cards.
- Number cue cards in top right corner.
- Mark cards with colour symbols indicating need for visual aid.
- Fasten the cards loosely together by punching a hole in the top right-hand corner of each and tying with string. That way if you drop them you can pick all the cards up without difficulty.

USING VISUAL AIDS WITH YOUR MESSAGE

- Have only *one* idea per visual. Choose your words carefully, the fewer the better. Brief bullet points are easier to read than long lines of text.
- Underline the title. Separate each point with a number.
- Make sure every visual has a message. Never show pictures, charts or tables unless they are *essential* to the point being made.
- Use colours to catch the audience's attention.

- Explain the visual. Maintain eye contact with your listeners while doing so. Never talk to the flip chart, screen or OHP.
- Never turn your back on the audience. With a large group, read the visual aloud to ensure everybody understands it.
- Ensure your hand-outs have a polished look. The typing must be neat and the grammar and spelling flawless.
- If using models, make notes and fix them to the back of the models as an aid to memory.
- Practise revealing the OHP transparency on cue with the content of your speech.
- Keep the projector switched off until you are ready to reveal the transparency. Or use a large sheet of card or thick paper to black out the entire screen until you are ready.
- Use blanks in the 35 mm projector tray at the start and end of a set of slides.
- Never remove a transparency from the OHP while it is switched on.
- When not on the OHP, a fiche should be easy to read at six feet.
- Use upper and lower case letters rather than all capitals, as they are easier to read.
- Never write vertically on the fiche as it is hard to read.
- Use dark colours such as red, black, blue or green rather than orange, yellow or light brown.
- Mix different colours and type styles to highlight contrasting ideas.
- Make brief notes on the card mounts of OHP transparencies. Position these so you can read them easily while you are facing the audience.
- To avoid projecting odd-shaped images on the screen, tilt it towards or away from the projector. If the top of the image is wider than the bottom tilt the top of the

screen towards the projector. If the bottom of the image is too wide, move the top of the screen away from the projector.

- Isolate parts of the OHP using a sheet of paper. You will be able to read the next point through a normal weight sheet with the projector switched on.
- If you plan to write on the OHP transparency, practise neat handwriting. Large, thick writing appears confident while small, thin, script makes you look weak.
- Pre-write notes on the border then copy them out. Only you will know what is being done!
- OHPs are best with audiences of 10–400. Do not bother when presenting to less than 10—use hand-outs instead. Always have a back-up OHP or one with two light bulbs.
- Remember the 6x rule. The distance of the furthest member of your audience should never be more than six times the width of the projection screen.
- Stand to the right of the projection screen (from the audience's viewpoint) so that after reading your slide their eyes will come to rest on you.

GETTING YOUR MESSAGE ACROSS NON-VERBALLY

- Be sure to make eye contact with your whole audience. Do not ignore those seated at the side or back of the room.
- Avoid fidgeting—it only distracts your listeners.
- Remember everybody looks more confident than they often feel.
- Stand up whenever possible. We pay more attention to people who speak while standing up than those who are seated. If necessary have an excuse to stand, i.e. passing around notes.

- At the start, tilt your head forwards slightly. Smile. Look slowly around the room.
- 'Plant' yourself with your weight distributed equally between both legs.
- Keep your back straight but relaxed to allow a smooth air flow into the lungs.
- Keep your chin tilted slightly up to direct your voice towards your listeners rather than the floor.
- Use gestures if these feel natural to you.
- Men should avoid placing their hands in their trouser pockets since it looks slovenly. If you do want to do so, keep them still!

Where to Find What You Need to Know

There are two main sources for researching an important new presentation:

- Published records available to anybody who knows where to look and what to look for;
- Personal information obtained over the telephone or through face-to-face conversations.

Finding your way around published records requires knowledge and patience. Making the most of face-to-face or telephone conversations demands listening skills plus a knowledge of what questions to ask and when to ask them.

PUBLISHED SOURCES

Business Directories

These will tell you what achievements, if any, are credited to your potential customer. If he or she has written books or articles you should have at least a passing knowledge of them prior to the first meeting.

Business Press

This includes such general interest business publications as *Fortune*, *International Business Week*, *Harvard Business Review*, Sloane newspapers such as the *Financial Times* (UK) and *Wall Street Journal* (US), together with the business pages of serious newspapers.

Clip and file articles from relevant magazines and newspapers on a regular basis, not only about companies of immediate concern but in the general area of your business interests, for instance computing, electronics, finance, retailing and so on. Cuttings are placed in a folder which can be read at your convenience, perhaps when travelling by train or plane.

Keep yourself well informed about world trends likely to affect business by including news magazines such as *Time*, *Newsweek* and *The Economist* as part of your regular weekly reading.

Business Information on Cassettes

A useful service for keeping busy executives up to date with all the latest trends and discoveries is offered by a New Jersey-based company, Newstrack American Tape Service (700 Black Horse Pike, Blackwood, NJ 08012). They extract and record on cassettes articles and features from a wide variety of business sources.

279

Business Information on Disc and CD-ROM

Many relevant sources are now available on computer disc or CD-ROM. Although the investment required to set up such a service is fairly high, CD-ROMs provide a fast and convenient method of searching for a large amount of data.

Business Information on Computer Database

Many business-related magazines are available through on-line databases, for example FT Profile (UK), Lexus/Nexis, Newsnet, Dow Jones News/Retrieval, or CompuServe.

These specialist news and information databases typically allow access to a wide range of sources, including wire services, Dow Jones, TASS and Associated Press, most major newsletter and company reports as well as such services as Reuters Textline, Global Scan, Nikkei, ICC and Infocheck.

Some publishers now make their publications available through databases, including McGraw-Hill which offers full-text, unedited articles from more than 45 technical publications covering fields as diverse as plastics and chemical engineering, coal and petrochemicals, securities and data communications.

Industrial Research Firms

Companies such as Mintel and credit checkers such as CCN (UK) and America's MDS Group provide a wide range of information about prospective customers, including their credit worthiness.

Fortune magazine offers a research service by fax, Fortune Company Profiles, covering thousands of US public companies, compiled from dozens of sources including Reuters and Standard and Poor's Disclosure. This can be faxed anywhere in the world.

Virtually every type of business in the world now has at least one magazine or newsletter devoted to their concerns.

Local Newspapers

Even minor events and activities for companies in their circulation area are likely to be reported by the local newspaper. However, unless you are doing major research on a company, it is seldom worth investing the time and effort necessary to track down relevant stories.

House Journals

Most large organisations publish their own house journals which can often be obtained by a direct request to the public relations or press office of the company concerned.

They provide a wealth of fascinating and invaluable information on products, achievements, promotions and company personnel.

Apart from their factual content, such journals give you a feel for corporate culture. Are they entertaining, even slightly irreverent, off-beat and creative, or plodding and worthy but devoid of wit? The chances are their style reflects the culture of that company and the attitudes of senior management. Take such differences into account when preparing your message.

Dropping information gleaned from such sources into a preliminary conversation with the prospective customers can be a fast way of putting yourself on their side.

PERSONAL SOURCES

Specialists

Cultivate people with insider knowledge of your industry. Talk to trade and business journalists, stockbrokers and analysts who cover that sector.

Telephone Calls

This is an extremely powerful research tool which, when used correctly, allows you to bypass people such as secretaries, receptionists and personal assistants who—if dealt with face to face—might prove significant obstacles to obtaining the knowledge you require.

Failed Presentations

Even the best presentations will not always succeed in winning you new business. While failure is never welcome, it can provide a valuable learning experience, teaching you how to avoid similar pitfalls and problems in the future.

Remember that information gathered about your audience is an indispensable guide to the decisions you will be making about every aspect of your presentation.

Your audience is a final arbiter and how well you have adapted your material to focus on the needs, experiences and attitudes of your listeners will determine whether your presentation soars or sinks.

If you have not already done so, start a cuttings library in your relevant sector of interest. Read as many general and specific business and trade publications as possible.

Aim to invest at least 5 per cent of your income on self-improvement, by subscribing to magazines, journals, buying books and taking courses.

Index